1,000 Quotes
For Writers
...inspiration for your creative writing

Kimberly Coleman

crassus

ISBN-10: 0991413261
ISBN-13: 978-0-9914132-6-3

Photo Credits:
Cover Photo © Epitavi www.fotosearch.com
Title Page Photo © worac www.fotosearch.com
'summer' girl in field © Mallivan www.fotosearch.com
'truth' armor rose © Zinkevych www.fotosearch.com
'life & love' perfect rose © Korionov www.fotosearch.com
'unforgettable' woman in lace © iordani www.fotosearch.com
Other Photos are Public Domain Courtesy of Pixabay and Wikipedia

Cover and Interior Design by Kimberly Coleman

This volume is dedicated to the writers
who strive every day to give voice
to their stories and dreams.

*"The living owe it to those who no longer can speak
to tell their story for them."*
— *Czesław Miłosz, **The Issa Valley***

table of contents

foreword

There once was a time when writers met doing exciting things: climbing Mt. Everest, big game safaris in the Serengeti, or exploring the mystic arts of ancient Egypt. At least, that's how they said they met. It could be that the egos in play didn't want to admit they met lying in a gutter outside a pub in a bad part of London or their penny farthings collided because no one could steer those things.

The truth isn't always pretty or saleable.

I met Kimberly Coleman on Twitter. She's yet another in an increasingly long line of friends I'll likely never meet face-to-face. That's okay, though, because even though we didn't meet exploring Khmer temples or fighting off a new and exciting plague, we did meet and that's better than not meeting. That truth may not exciting, but it's the truth.

So, what does Twitter have to do with a book about quotes for writing? Well, a couple things, actually. Twitter is a good place to meet people; you'll come across some scary folk, but there are good people out there. A good quote can introduce you to an author you've never met. Think of it as a buddy who's introducing you to another buddy. Also, a good quote is a like a good tweet: you may have to wade through a sea of refuse, but when you find that one good tweet it sticks with you. That one good quote can change your whole day or your whole outlook.

*There may only be a few words in a good quote, but those few words can be important. **1,000 Quotes For Writers** isn't one of those books you're meant to read in one sitting. Like a fine Scotch, books about quotes are meant to be sipped and enjoyed over a long period.*

When you start writing, you start finding inspiration everywhere. Quotes, especially the great ones, can tell an entire story in a few words. That story may not be obvious in the quote itself, but the great quote — like the great tweet — can unlock an idea and point you in the right direction or lay the groundwork of what will one day become the next great novel.

— Eric Lahti
Author of **The Henchmen Series**

*"Quotes are like seeds that merge with
other seeds and create a unique
orchard in each fertile mind."*
— *Ebal*

summer

summer

*"Summer afternoon....summer afternoon; to me those
have always been the two most beautiful words in
the English language."*
— Henry James

*"'People run away to be alone,' he said. 'Some people
had to be alone.'"*
— William Trevor, **Love and Summer**

*"In the summer evenings, fireflies swarm around the tarn,
making something hateful almost beautiful."*
— Bethany Griffin, **The Fall**

*"He loved her, he loved her, and until he'd loved her she
had never minded being alone...."*
— Truman Capote, **Summer Crossing**

*"Lovers and madmen have such seething brains
Such shaping fantasies, that apprehend
More than cool reason ever comprehends."*
— William Shakespeare,
A Midsummer Night's Dream

*"In the depth of winter, I finally learned that
there was in me an invincible summer."*
— Albert Camus

"The weeks stood still in summer...."
— Rainer Maria Rilke

"I know I am but summer to your heart, and not the full four seasons of the year."
— *Edna St. Vincent Millay*

"It was one of those March days when the sun shines hot and the wind blows cold: when it is summer in the light, and winter in the shade."
— *Charles Dickens,* **Great Expectations**

"One swallow does not make a summer, neither does one fine day..."
— *Aristotle*

"If it could only be like this always — always summer, always alone, the fruit always ripe and Aloysius in a good temper..."
— *Evelyn Waugh,* **Brideshead Revisited**

"I don't know how long I kept at it...I felt reasonably safe, stretched out on the floor, and lay quite still. It didn't seem to be summer anymore..."
— *Sylvia Plath,* **The Bell Jar**

"Fantasy tastes of habaneros and honey, cinnamon and cloves, rare red meat and wines as sweet as summer. Reality is beans and tofu, and ashes at the end."
— *George R.R. Martin*

"Summer's lease hath all too short a date."
— *William Shakespeare*

reading

reading

"One day, you will be old enough to start reading fairytales again."
— *C.S. Lewis,* **The Chronicles of Narnia**

"Her reputation for reading a great deal hung about her like the cloudy envelope of a goddess in an epic."
— *Henry James,* **The Portrait of a Lady**

"If one cannot enjoy reading a book over and over again, there is no use in reading it at all."
— *Oscar Wilde*

"How much sooner one tires of anything than of a book! When I have a house of my own, I shall be miserable if I have not an excellent library."
— *Jane Austen,* **Pride and Prejudice**

"You don't have to burn books to destroy a culture. Just get people to stop reading them."
— *Ray Bradbury*

"Writing in English is the most ingenious torture ever devised for sins committed in previous lives. The English reading public explains the reason why."
— *James Joyce*

"The world was hers for the reading."
— *Betty Smith,* **A Tree Grows in Brooklyn**

"People can lose their lives in libraries. They ought to be warned."
— *Saul Bellow*

"Books are the plane, and the train, and the road. They are the destination, and the journey. They are home."
— *Anna Quindlen,*
How Reading Changed My Life

"Writing comes from reading, and reading is the finest teacher of how to write."
— *Annie Proulx*

"I am too fond of reading books to care to write them."
— *Oscar Wilde,* **The Picture of Dorian Gray**

"Reading is the sole means by which we slip, involuntarily, often helplessly, into another's skin, another's voice, another's soul."
— *Joyce Carol Oates*

"What really knocks me out is a book that, when you're all done reading it, you wish the author that wrote it was a terrific friend of yours and you could call him up on the phone whenever you felt like it."
— *J.D. Salinger,* **The Catcher in the Rye**

"There are worse crimes than burning books. One of them is not reading them."
— *Joseph Brodsky*

friendship

friendship

"Don't walk in front of me...I may not follow
Don't walk behind me...I may not lead
Walk beside me...just be my friend."
— Albert Camus

"Do I not destroy my enemies when I make them
my friends?"
— Abraham Lincoln

"Good friends, good books, and a sleepy conscience: this
is the ideal life."
— Mark Twain

"It is not a lack of love, but a lack of friendship that
makes unhappy marriages."
— Friedrich Nietzsche

"If you live to be a hundred, I want to live to be a hundred
minus one day so I never have to live without you."
— Joan Powers, **Pooh's Little Instruction Book**

"'Why did you do all this for me?' he asked. 'I don't
deserve it. I've never done anything for you.'
'You have been my friend,' replied Charlotte.
'That in itself is a tremendous thing.'"
— E.B. White, **Charlotte's Web**

"No person is your friend who demands your silence,
or denies your right to grow."
— Alice Walker

"There is no surer foundation for a beautiful friendship than a mutual taste in literature."
— *P.G. Wodehouse*

"You are my best friend as well as my lover, and I do not know which side of you I enjoy the most. I treasure each side, just as I have treasured our life together."
— *Nicholas Sparks,* **The Notebook**

"Friendship is unnecessary, like philosophy, like art... It has no survival value; rather it is one of those things which give value to survival."
— *C.S. Lewis,* **The Four Loves**

"Each friend represents a world in us, a world possibly not born until they arrive, and it is only by this meeting that a new world is born."
— *Anaïs Nin*

"'Why is it,' he said, one time, at the subway entrance, 'I feel I've known you so many years?' 'Because I like you,' she said, 'and I don't want anything from you.'"
— *Ray Bradbury,* **Fahrenheit 451**

"Words are easy, like the wind; faithful friends are hard to find."
— *William Shakespeare*

"A friend is someone who knows all about you and still loves you."
— *Elbert Hubbard*

life

life

"Either we live by accident and die by accident, or we live by plan and die by plan."
— Thornton Wilder, **The Bridge of San Luis Rey**

"Saying nothing sometimes says the most."
— Emily Dickinson

"Life begins on the other side of despair."
— Jean-Paul Sartre

"What are clouds, but an excuse for the sky? What is life, but an escape from death?"
— James Clavell

*"At the door of life, by the gate of breath,
There are worse things waiting for men than death."*
— Algernon Charles Swinburne

"It's time to start living the life you've imagined."
— Henry James

"Man's loneliness is but his fear of life."
— Eugene O'Neill

"Do any human beings ever realize life while they live it?"
— Thornton Wilder, **Our Town**

"Anxiety is the handmaiden of creativity."
— T.S. Eliot

"A person's life isn't orderly...it runs about all over the place, in and out through time. The present's hardly there; the future doesn't exist. Only love matters in the bits and pieces of a person's life."
— William Trevor

"Life, although it may only be an accumulation of anguish, is dear to me, and I will defend it."
— Mary Shelley, **Frankenstein**

"Every life is in many days, day after day. We walk through ourselves, meeting robbers, ghosts, giants, old men, young men, wives, widows, brothers-in-love, but always meeting ourselves."
— James Joyce, **Ulysses**

"A life spent making mistakes is not only more honorable, but more useful than a life spent doing nothing."
— George Bernard Shaw

"I am little concerned with beauty or perfection. I don't care for the great centuries. All I care about is life, struggle, intensity."
— Émile Zola

"Three things in human life are important: the first is to be kind; the second is to be kind; and the third is to be kind."
— Henry James

"Every monster was a man first."
— Edward Albee, **Tiny Alice**

on writing...

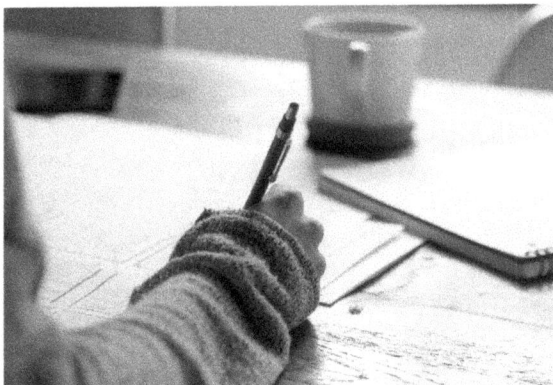

on writing...

"Writing is my vacation from living."
— *Eugene O'Neill*

*"To me, the greatest pleasure of writing is not what it's about,
but the music the words make."*
— *Truman Capote*

*"It's hell writing and it's hell not writing. The only tolerable state
is having just written."*
— *Robert Hass*

*"Writing is supposed to be difficult, agonizing, a dreadful exercise,
a terrible occupation."*
— *Ray Bradbury,* **Zen in the Art of Writing**

*"People like me write because otherwise we are pretty inarticulate.
Our articulation is our writing."*
— *William Trevor*

"Writing is the great invention of the world."
— *Abraham Lincoln*

*"Writing is like breathing, it's possible to learn to do it well,
but the point is to do it no matter what."*
— *Julia Cameron*

"I can't really articulate what I feel."
— *Harold Pinter*

"What's writing really about? It's about trying to take fuller possession of the reality of your life."
— Ted Hughes

"I almost always urge people to write in the first person. Writing is an act of ego and you might as well admit it."
— William Zinsser

"You should write because you love the shape of stories and sentences and the creation of different words on a page."
— Annie Proulx

"You are always naked when you start writing; you are always as if you had never written anything before; you are always a beginner. Shakespeare wrote without knowing he would become Shakespeare."
— Erica Jong

"The privilege is not writing a novel, it's to have someone read it. When you look at it that way, you realize the responsibility you have to put your very best on the page."
— Javier A. Robayo

"What do you want? What are you willing to give up to get it? Writing requires you make sacrifices. Be prepared to work hard to be a writer."
— Sandra Brown

"I have the defect of being more sincere than persons wish."
— Molière, **The Misanthrope**

the poets

the poets

"We delight in the beauty of the butterfly, but rarely admit the changes it has gone through to achieve that beauty."
— *Maya Angelou*

"I shut my eyes and all the world drops dead;
I lift my eyes and all is born again."
— *Sylvia Plath*

"I love you as certain dark things are to be loved,
in secret, between the shadow and the soul."
— *Pablo Neruda,* **100 Love Sonnets**

"Everything is complicated; if that were not so, life and poetry and everything else would be a bore."
— *Wallace Stevens*

"What is that you express in your eyes? It seems to me more than all the print I have read in my life."
— *Walt Whitman*

"Poetry is what happens when nothing else can."
— *Charles Bukowski*

"Poetry might be defined as the clear expression of mixed feelings."
— *W.H. Auden,* **New Year Letter**

"I have defined poetry as a 'passionate pursuit of the Real.'"
— *Czesław Miłosz*

"Love consists of this: two solitudes that meet, protect and greet each other."
— *Rainer Maria Rilke*

"What happens in the heart, simply happens."
— *Ted Hughes*

"The possible's slow fuse is lit by the Imagination."
— *Emily Dickinson*

"My imagination is a monastery, and I am its monk."
— *John Keats*

"Can you tell me aught of England or of Spring in England now?"
— *Rudyard Kipling*

"Resist much, obey little."
— *Walt Whitman,* **Leaves of Grass**

"Unbeing dead isn't being alive."
— *e.e. cummings*

"Grow old with me! The best is yet to be."
— *Robert Browning*

peace

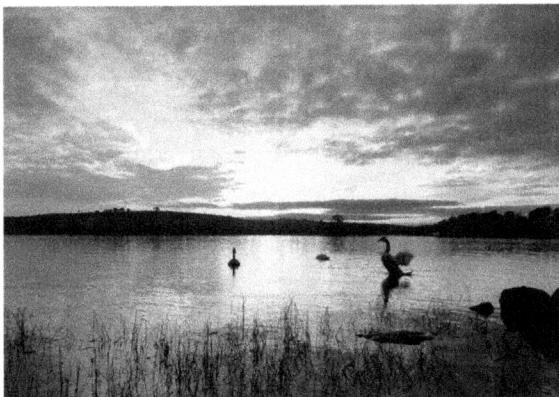

peace

"Let the peace of this day be here tomorrow when I wake up."
— *Thomas Pynchon,* **Gravity's Rainbow**

*"If everyone fought for their own convictions there would
be no war."*
— *Leo Tolstoy,* **War and Peace**

*"I loved her against reason, against promise, against peace,
against hope, against happiness, against all discouragement
that could be."*
— *Charles Dickens,* **Great Expectations**

*"You can have peace. Or you can have freedom. Don't ever
count on having both at once."*
— *Robert A. Heinlein*

*"It is not enough to win a war; it is more important to
organize the peace."*
— *Aristotle*

"You cannot find peace by avoiding life."
— *Virginia Woolf*

"Nothing can bring you peace but yourself."
— *Ralph Waldo Emerson*

"Remember your humanity, and forget the rest."
— *Bertrand Russell*

"Go in the direction of where your peace is coming from."
— C. JoyBell C.

"To sit with a dog on a hillside on a glorious afternoon is to be back in Eden, where doing nothing was not boring — it was peace."
— Milan Kundera

"Peace? Ah, yes, defined as a period of time to allow for preparation for the next war."
— Terry Pratchett, **Unseen Academicals**

"Peace cannot be achieved through violence, it can only be attained through understanding."
— Ralph Waldo Emerson

"We shall find peace. We shall hear angels, we shall see the sky sparkling with diamonds."
— Anton Chekhov

"I still believe that peace and plenty and happiness can be worked out some way. I am a fool."
— Kurt Vonnegut

"Obsessed by a fairy tale, we spend our lives searching for a magic door and a lost kingdom of peace."
— Eugene O'Neill

"The peace which I always found in the silence and emptiness of the moors filled me utterly."
— James Herriot

life again...

life again...

*"There are two tragedies in life. One is to lose your heart's
desire. The other is to gain it."*
— *George Bernard Shaw,* **Man and Superman**

*"There are few hours in life more agreeable than the hour
dedicated to the ceremony known as afternoon tea."*
— *Henry James,* **The Portrait of a Lady**

*"Moments of their secret life together burst like stars
upon his memory."*
— *James Joyce,* **The Dead**

"Life is a solitary cell whose walls are mirrors."
— *Eugene O'Neill*

*"If I have learned anything in this long life of mine, it is this:
in love, we find out who we want to be;
in war, we find out who we are."*
— *Kristin Hannah,* **The Nightingale**

*"...I know nothing of life but despair, death, fear,
and fatuous superficiality cast over an abyss of sorrow.
I see how peoples are set against one another, and in
silence, unknowingly, foolishly, obediently, innocently
slay one another."*
— *Erich Maria Remarque*

"A good book is an event in my life."
— *Stendhal,* **The Red and the Black**

"Literature is the most agreeable way of ignoring life."
— *Fernando Pessoa,* **The Book of Disquiet**

"But, in her life, nothing was going to happen. Such was the will of God! The future was a dark corridor, and at the far end the door was bolted."
— *Gustave Flaubert,* **Madame Bovary**

"That's why I write, because life never works except in retrospect. You can't control life, at least you can control your version."
— *Chuck Palahniuk,* **Stranger than Fiction**

"Set your life on fire. Seek those who fan your flames."
— *Jalaluddin Rumi*

"In order to write about life first you must live it."
— *Ernest Hemingway*

"Writing is my life. Life is my hobby."
— *Emma Lai*

"It was easy enough to kill yourself in a fit of despair. It was easy enough to play the martyr. It was harder to do nothing. To endure your life. To wait."
— *Erica Jong*

the Russians

the Russians

"The illusion which exalts us is dearer to us than ten
thousand truths."
— *Aleksandr Pushkin*

"Literature is the art of discovering something extraordinary
about ordinary people, and saying with ordinary words
something extraordinary."
— *Boris Pasternak*

"My turn shall also come:
I sense the spreading of a wing."
— *Osip Mandelstam,* **The Selected Poem**

"When truth is replaced by silence, the silence is a lie."
— *Yevgeny Yevtushenko*

"Days follow days in flight, and every day is taking
Fragments of being, while together you and I
Make plans to live..."
— *Aleksandr Pushkin*

"I don't like people who have never fallen or stumbled. Their
virtue is lifeless and it isn't of much value. Life hasn't
revealed its beauty to them."
— *Boris Pasternak*

"Everything is moved by love."
— *Osip Mandelstam,* **Stone**

*"Habit is Heaven's own redress: it takes the place
of happiness."*
— Aleksandr Pushkin

*"When a great moment knocks on the door of your life,
it is often no louder than the beating of your heart, and
it is very easy to miss it."*
— Boris Pasternak

"I love my poor earth because I have seen no other."
— Osip Mandelstam

*"A poet's autobiography is his poetry. Anything else
is just a footnote."*
— Yevgeny Yevtushenko

*"If you but knew the flames that burn in me which I attempt
to beat down with my reason."*
— Aleksandr Pushkin

*"I have the impression that if he didn't complicate his life so
needlessly, he would die of boredom."*
— Boris Pasternak, Doctor Zhivago

*"I envy everyone secretly,
I secretly love everything."*
— Osip Mandelstam, **The Selected Poems**

*"All values in this world are, more or less, questionable,
but the most important thing in life is human kindness."*
— Yevgeny Yevtushenko

youth

youth

"My dreams, my dreams! What has become of their sweetness?
What indeed has become of my youth?"
— *Aleksandr Pushkin,* **Eugene Onegin**

"Childhood is the kingdom where nobody dies. Nobody that
matters, that is."
— *Edna St. Vincent Millay*

"Summer will end soon enough, and childhood as well."
— *George R.R. Martin,* **A Game of Thrones**

"The soul is healed by being with children."
— *Fyodor Dostoyevsky*

"Rules are for children. This is war, and in war the only
crime is to lose."
— *Joe Abercrombie,* **Last Argument of Kings**

"Do not read, as children do, to amuse yourself, or like the
ambitious, for the purpose of instruction. No,
read in order to live."
— *Gustave Flaubert*

"Youth is easily deceived because it is quick to hope."
— *Aristotle*

"Every man should lose a battle in his youth, so he
does not lose a war when he is old."
— *George R.R. Martin,* **A Feast for Crows**

"Children see magic because they look for it."
— Christopher Moore

"Youth is a dream, a form of chemical madness."
— F. Scott Fitzgerald

"What a weary time those years were...to have the desire and the need to live but not the ability."
— Charles Bukowski

"The surest way to corrupt a youth is to instruct him to hold in higher esteem those who think alike than those who think differently."
— Friedrich Nietzsche

"Youth is happy because it has the capacity to see beauty. Anyone who keeps the ability to see beauty never grows old."
— Franz Kafka

"I was not a hypocrite, with one real face and several false ones. I had several faces because I was young and didn't know who I was or wanted to be."
— Milan Kundera

"The secret of remaining young is never to have an emotion that is unbecoming."
— Oscar Wilde, **The Picture of Dorian Gray**

"Keep true to the dreams of thy youth."
— Friedrich Schiller

night

& day

night & day

"The darker the night, the brighter the stars,
The deeper the grief, the closer is God!"
— *Fyodor Dostoyevsky,* **Crime and Punishment**

"Today will die tomorrow."
— *Algernon Charles Swinburne*

"We are what we pretend to be, so we must be careful about
what we pretend to be."
— *Kurt Vonnegut,* **Mother Night**

"There is only one day left, always starting over: it is
given to us at dawn and taken away from us at dusk."
— *Jean-Paul Sartre*

"I have loved the stars too fondly to be fearful of the night."
— *Sarah Williams*

"Seek the lofty by reading, hearing and seeing great work
at some moment, every day."
— *Thornton Wilder*

"Just stay with the pale moon
when darkness wants the night to be brave."
— *Munia Khan*

"History...is a nightmare from which I am trying to awake."
— *James Joyce,* **Ulysses**

"But how could you live and have no story to tell?"
— Fyodor Dostoyevsky, **White Nights**

"Did not one spend the first half of one's days in dreams of happiness and the second half in regrets and terrors?"
— Émile Zola, **The Joy of Life**

"To be Despair. It is a portrait. Only close your eyes and feel."
— Neil Gaiman, **The Sandman: Endless Nights**

"They wrote in the old days that it is sweet and fitting to die for one's country. But in modern war, there is nothing sweet nor fitting in your dying. You will die like a dog for no good reason."
— Ernest Hemingway

"I've always loved the night, when everyone else is asleep and the world is all mine. It's quiet and dark — the perfect time for creativity."
— Jonathan Harnisch, **Porcelain Utopia**

"I have drunken deep of joy, And I will taste no other wine tonight."
— Percy Bysshe Shelley

"If you shut up truth and bury it under the ground, it will but grow, and gather to itself such explosive power that the day it bursts through it will blow up everything in its way."
— Émile Zola

happiness

happiness

"Man only likes to count his troubles; he doesn't calculate his happiness."
— *Fyodor Dostoyevsky*, **Notes from Underground**

"All happiness depends on courage and work."
— *Honoré de Balzac*

"*It's a great game — the pursuit of happiness."*
— *Eugene O'Neill*

"I have but one passion: to enlighten those who have been kept in the dark, in the name of humanity which has suffered so much and is entitled to happiness. My fiery protest is simply the cry of my very soul."
— *Émile Zola*

"Once again...welcome to my house. Come freely. Go safely, and leave something of the happiness you bring."
— *Bram Stoker*, **Dracula**

"Happiness quite unshared can scarcely be called happiness; it has no taste."
— *Charlotte Brontë*

"Unhappiness is the ultimate form of self-indulgence."
— *Tom Robbins*

"A man is happy so long as he chooses to be happy."
— *Aleksandr Solzhenitsyn,* **Cancer Ward**

"Even if there were only two men left in the world and both of them saints they wouldn't be happy. One of them would be bound to try and improve the other. That is the nature of things."
— *Frank O'Connor*

"If people can just love each other a little bit, they can be so happy."
— *Émile Zola,* **Germinal**

"Much unhappiness has come into the world because of bewilderment and things left unsaid."
— *Fyodor Dostoyevsky*

"You will never be happy if you continue to search for what happiness consists of. You will never live if you are looking for the meaning of life."
— *Albert Camus*

"No medicine cures what happiness cannot."
— *Gabriel García Márquez*

"Let us be grateful to the people who make us happy; they are the charming gardeners who make our souls blossom."
— *Marcel Proust*

words

lity has its limits; the world of ·
boundless."
— Jean-Jacques Rousseau

ge people to write in the first pers
ego and you might as well admit
— William Zinsser

rite in a clear style, let him be fi
thoughts; and if any
: noble style, let him first possess
— Johann Wolfgang von Goethe

ublished writer, I remained comp·
rite and courses on the subject...
' style; made me observe caution; ·
me with rules."

words

"Music expresses that which cannot be put into words and that which cannot remain silent."
— *Victor Hugo*

"Words are all we have."
— *Samuel Beckett*

"You see how I try
To reach with words
What matters most
And how I fail."
— *Czesław Miłosz*

"Raise your words, not voice. It is rain that grows flowers, not thunder."
— *Jalaluddin Rumi*

"However stupid a fool's words may be, they are sometimes enough to confound an intelligent man."
— *Nikolai Gogol,* **Dead Souls**

"Own only what you can always carry with you: know languages, know countries, know people. Let your memory be your travel bag."
— *Aleksandr Solzhenitsyn*

"War is what happens when language fails."
— *Margaret Atwood*

"If you have the words, there's always a chance that you'll find the way."
— Seamus Heaney

"The words 'I Love You' kill, and resurrect millions, in less than a second."
— Aberjhani,
Elemental: The Power of Illuminated Love

"A thousand words leave not the same deep impression as does a single deed."
— Henrik Ibsen

"Bare lists of words are found suggestive to an imaginative and excited mind."
— Ralph Waldo Emerson

"Music is the universal language of mankind."
— Henry Wadsworth Longfellow

"'Without the gods, how would I sing?' I asked. 'With your own voice,' he said."
— Erica Jong, **Sappho's Leap**

"When asked, 'Why do you always wear black?', he said, 'I am mourning for my life.'"
— Anton Chekhov

"Language is the only homeland."
— Czesław Miłosz

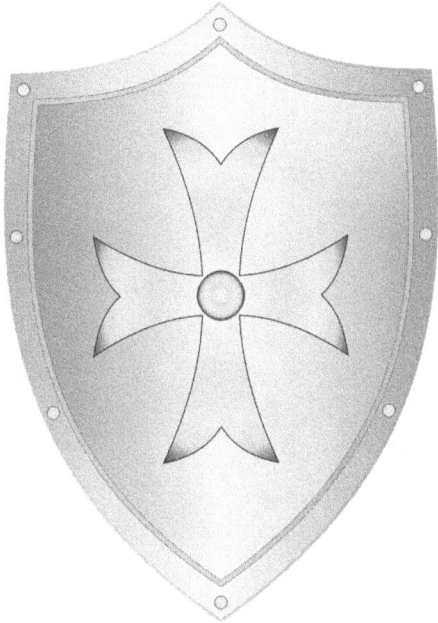

war

war

"Imagination is the only weapon in the war against reality."
— *Lewis Carroll,* **Alice in Wonderland**

*"War must be, while we defend our lives against a destroyer
who would devour all; but I do not love the bright sword
for its sharpness, nor the arrow for its swiftness, nor the warrior
for his glory. I love only that which they defend."*
— *J.R.R. Tolkien,* **The Two Towers**

"Only the dead have seen the end of war."
— *Plato*

*"All war is a symptom of man's failure as a
thinking animal."*
— *John Steinbeck*

"A state of war only serves as an excuse for domestic tyranny."
— *Aleksandr Solzhenitsyn*

"When the rich wage war it's the poor who die."
— *Jean-Paul Sartre*

*"Never think that war, no matter how necessary, nor how
justified, is not a crime."*
— *Ernest Hemingway*

"In wars, boy, fools kill other fools for foolish causes."
— *Robert Jordan,* **To the Blight**

"For the dead and the living, we must bear witness."
— Elie Wiesel

"...And when all the wars are over, a butterfly will still be beautiful."
— Ruskin Bond, **Scenes from a Writer's Life**

"In times of war, the law falls silent."
— Marcus Tullius Cicero

"If we don't end war, war will end us."
— H.G. Wells

"Religion isn't the cause of wars, it's the excuse."
— Jasper Fforde, **The Eyre Affair**

"And if we burn, you burn with us."
— Suzanne Collins, **Mockingjay**

"Cry havoc and let slip the dogs of war!"
— William Shakespeare, **Julius Caesar**

"The enemy is anybody who's going to get you killed, no matter which side he is on."
— Joseph Heller, **Catch-22**

"It is forbidden to kill; therefore, all murderers are punished unless they kill in large numbers and to the sound of trumpets."
— Voltaire

reading again...

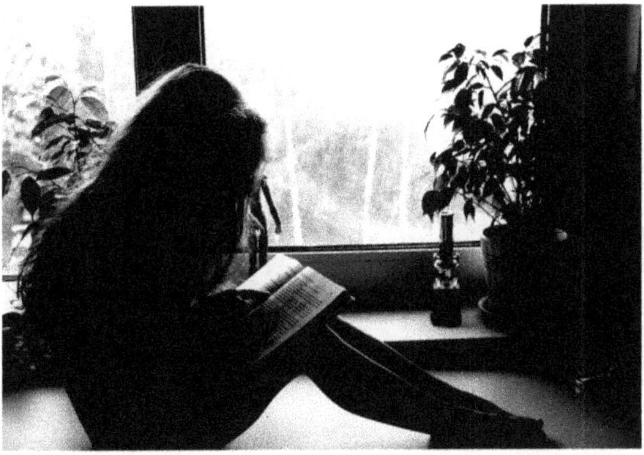

reading again...

"Sleep is good, he said, and books are better."
— George R.R. Martin

"If you don't have time to read, you don't have the time
(or the tools) to write. Simple as that."
— Stephen King

"The books that the world calls immoral are books that
show the world its own shame."
— Oscar Wilde, **The Picture of Dorian Gray**

"'Classic': a book which people praise and don't read."
— Mark Twain

"You can never get a cup of tea large enough or a book
long enough to suit me."
— C.S. Lewis

"We read to know we're not alone."
— William Nicholson, **Shadowlands**

"Sometimes, you read a book and it fills you with this weird
evangelical zeal, and you become convinced that the shattered
world will never be put back together unless and until
all living humans read the book."
— John Green, **The Fault in Our Stars**

"Until I feared I would lose it, I never loved to read.
One does not love breathing."
— Harper Lee, **To Kill a Mockingbird**

"A great book should leave you with many experiences,
and slightly exhausted at the end. You live several lives
while reading."
— William Styron

"Let us read, and let us dance; these two amusements
will never do any harm to the world."
— Voltaire

"Think before you speak. Read before you think."
— Fran Lebowitz

"No tears in the writer, no tears in the reader. No surprise
in the writer, no surprise in the reader."
— Robert Frost

"Read, read, read. Read everything...trash, classics, good
and bad, and see how they do it. Just like a carpenter who
works as an apprentice and studies the master. Read!
You'll absorb it. Then write."
— William Faulkner

"If you would tell me the heart of a man, tell me not what he
reads, but what he rereads."
— François Mauriac

the British

the British

"I'm glad you like adverbs — I adore them; they are the only qualifications I really much respect."
— Henry James

"He's more myself than I am. Whatever our souls are made of, his and mine are the same."
— Emily Brontë, **Wuthering Heights**

"Like the British Constitution, she owes her success in practice to her inconsistencies in principle."
— Thomas Hardy

"Like all young men, you greatly exaggerate the difference between one young woman and another."
— George Bernard Shaw, **Major Barbara**

"It's a complex fate, being an American, and one of the responsibilities it entails is fighting against a superstitious valuation of Europe."
— Henry James

"If he loved with all the powers of his puny being, he couldn't love as much in eighty years as I could in a day."
— Emily Brontë, **Wuthering Heights**

"If the story-tellers could ha' got decency and good morals from true stories, who'd have troubled to invent parables?"
— Thomas Hardy, **Under the Greenwood Tree**

*"The single biggest problem in communication is the
illusion that it has taken place."*
— *George Bernard Shaw*

*"Sorrow comes in great waves...but rolls over us, and though
it may almost smother us, it leaves us. And we know that
if it is strong, we are stronger..."*
— *Henry James*

*"Be with me always — take any form — drive me mad! only
do not leave me in this abyss, where I cannot find you!
Oh, God! it is unutterable! I cannot live without my life!
I cannot live without my soul!"*
— *Emily Brontë,* **Wuthering Heights**

"But no one came. Because no one ever does."
— *Thomas Hardy,* **Jude the Obscure**

*"Make it a rule never to give a child a book you would
not read yourself."*
— *George Bernard Shaw*

*"I don't want everyone to like me; I should think less
of myself if some people did."*
— *Henry James*

"She burned too bright for this world."
— *Emily Brontë*

"A lover without indiscretion is no lover at all."
— *Thomas Hardy*

philosophical musings

philosophical musings

"Anger is really disappointed hope."
— Erica Jong

"The world of reality has its limits; the world of imagination is boundless."
— Jean-Jacques Rousseau

"Time spent with a cat is never wasted."
— Colette

"Why do people always expect authors to answer questions?
I am an author because I want to ask questions.
If I had answers, I'd be a politician."
— Eugène Ionesco

"She mediated, by turns, on broken promises and broken arches, phaetons and false hangings, Tilneys and trap-doors."
— Jane Austen

"I prefer thought to action, an idea to a transaction, contemplation to activity."
— Honoré de Balzac

"My fiction may, now and again, illuminate aspects of the human condition, but I do not consciously set out to do so: I am a storyteller."
— William Trevor

"Dance first. Think later. It's the natural order."
— Samuel Beckett

"A woman can become a man's friend only in the following stages: first an acquaintance, next a mistress, and only then a friend."
— Anton Chekhov, **The Three Sisters**

"You cannot have power for good without having power for evil, too. Even mother's milk nourishes murderers as well as heroes."
— George Bernard Shaw, **Major Barbara**

"All stories are ultimately about the fall."
— J.R.R. Tolkien

"Nothing is so painful to the human mind as a great and sudden change."
— Mary Shelley, **Frankenstein**

"Can miles truly separate you from friends...? If you want to be with someone you love, aren't you already there?"
— Richard Bach

"The whole conviction of my life now rests upon the belief that loneliness, far from being a rare and curious phenomenon, is the central and inevitable fact of human existence."
— Thomas Wolfe

people...

people...

"I get melancholy if I don't [write]. I need the company
of people who don't exist."
— William Trevor

"Taking a new step, uttering a new word, is what people
fear most."
— Fyodor Dostoyevsky

"If you want to tell people the truth, make them laugh,
otherwise they'll kill you."
— George Bernard Shaw

"People see what they think is there."
— Terry Pratchett

"It is always assumed by the empty-headed, who chatter
about themselves for want of something better, that people
who do not discuss their affairs openly must have
something to hide."
— Honoré de Balzac, **Père Goriot**

"I do not want people to be very agreeable, as it saves
me the trouble of liking them a great deal."
— Jane Austen, **Jane Austen's Letters**

"Dull people filled him with terror."
— Thomas Wolfe, **Look Homeward, Angel**

"You only have power over people as long as you don't take everything away from them. But when you've robbed a man of everything, he's no longer in your power: he's free again."
— Aleksandr Solzhenitsyn

"It is easy to love people in memory; the hard thing is to love them when they are there in front of you."
— John Updike

"I try to leave out the parts that people skip."
— Elmore Leonard

"Blessed are the weird people: poets, misfits, writers, mystics, painters, troubadours, for they teach us to see the world through different eyes."
— Jacob Nordby

"Writers aren't people exactly. Or, if they're any good, they're a whole lot of people trying so hard to be one person."
— F. Scott Fitzgerald

"Time, which changes people, does not alter the image we have of them."
— Marcel Proust

"Many people, myself among them, feel better at the mere sight of a book."
— Jane Smiley

love

love

"Love is space and time measured by the heart."
— *Marcel Proust*

"If I cannot inspire love, I will cause fear!"
— *Mary Shelley,* **Frankenstein**

"And remember this, that if you've been hated, you've also been loved."
— *Henry James,* **The Portrait of a Lady**

"The knowledge that she would never be loved in return acted upon her ideas as a tide acts upon cliffs."
— *Thornton Wilder,* **The Bridge of San Luis Rey**

"Perhaps one did not want to be loved so much as to be understood."
— *George Orwell,* **1984**

"Soul meets soul on lovers' lips."
— *Percy Bysshe Shelley*

"Goodbyes are only for those who love with their eyes. Because for those who love with heart and soul there is no such thing as separation."
— *Jalaluddin Rumi*

"Love loves to love love."
— *James Joyce,* **Ulysses**

"What is hell? I maintain that it is the suffering of being unable to love."
— *Fyodor Dostoyevsky,* **The Brothers Karamazov**

"Love is when you'd rather see someone one last time and die, than never see their face again."
— *Bryan Butvidas,* **Death of a True Love**

"Friends show their love in times of trouble, not in happiness."
— *Euripides*

"What a blessing it is to love books as I love them: to be able to converse with the dead, and to live amidst the unreal!"
— *Thomas Babington Macaulay*

"A thousand half-loves must be forsaken to take one whole heart home."
— *Jalaluddin Rumi*

"If this was love, love had been overrated."
— *Henry James,* **The Europeans**

"The true soldier fights not because he hates what is in front of him, but because he loves what is behind him."
— *G.K. Chesterton*

"You can love somebody without it being like that. You keep them a stranger, a stranger who's a friend."
— *Truman Capote,* **Breakfast at Tiffany's**

human

human

*"The whole conviction of my life now rests upon the belief
that loneliness, far from being a rare and curious phenomenon,
is the central and inevitable fact of human existence."*
— *Thomas Wolfe*

"Never say you know the last word about any human heart."
— *Henry James*

*"To believe you are magnificent.
And gradually to discover that
you are not magnificent.
Enough labor for one human life."*
— *Czesław Miłosz*

"Inability, human incapacity, is the only boundary to an art."
— *Émile Zola*

*"Show me a woman who doesn't feel guilty and I'll show
you a man."*
— *Erica Jong*

*"Wherever you come near the human race there's layers
and layers of nonsense."*
— *Thornton Wilder,* **Our Town**

*"Man is born broken. He lives by mending. The grace of
God is glue."*
— *Eugene O'Neill*

"I believe that before all else I am a reasonable human being, just as you are, or, at all events, that I must try and become one."
— *Henrik Ibsen,* **The Doll's House**

"A reader lives a thousand lives before he dies.... The man who never reads lives only one."
— *George R.R. Martin,*
A Dance with Dragons

"When a man is in despair, it means that he still believes in something."
— *Dmitri Shostakovich*

"Man will become better when you show him what he is like."
— *Anton Chekhov*

"The mystery of human existence lies not in just staying alive, but in finding something to live for."
— *Fyodor Dostoyevsky*

"Trust no friend without faults, and love a woman, but no angel."
— *Doris Lessing*

"Why is it that a woman can see from a distance what a man cannot see close?"
— *Thomas Hardy,*
The Return of the Native

the Victorians

the Victorians

*"Never close your lips to those whom you have already
opened your heart."*
— Charles Dickens

*"The tragedy of life is not so much what men suffer, but
rather what they miss."*
— Thomas Carlyle

"My sun sets to rise again."
— Robert Browning

"It is never too late to be what you might have been."
— George Eliot

*"I am longing to be with you, and by the sea, where we can
talk together freely and build our castles in the air."*
— Bram Stoker, Dracula

*"Suffering has been stronger than all other teaching, and has
taught me to understand what your heart used to be. I have
been bent and broken, but, I hope, into a better shape."*
— Charles Dickens, Great Expectations

*"No evil dooms us hopelessly except the evil we love, and
desire to continue in, and make no effort to escape from."*
— George Eliot

"A good book is the purest essence of a human soul."
— *Thomas Carlyle*

"Take away love and our earth is a tomb."
— *Robert Browning*

"Blessed is the man who, having nothing to say, abstains from giving us wordy evidence of the fact."
— *George Eliot*

"Remember my friend, that knowledge is stronger than memory, and we should not trust the weaker."
— *Bram Stoker, **Dracula***

"A man lives by believing something; not by debating and arguing about many things."
— *Thomas Carlyle*

"Fill your paper with the breathings of your heart."
— *William Wordsworth*

"I am all in a sea of wonders. I doubt; I fear; I think strange things, which I dare not confess to my own soul."
— *Bram Stoker, **Dracula***

"Have a heart that never hardens, and a temper that never tires, and a touch that never hurts."
— *Charles Dickens*

Babel, Gogol & Dostoyevsky

Babel, Gogol & Dostoyevsky

"If the world could write itself, it would write like Tolstoy."
— *Isaac Babel*

*"I am fated to journey hand in hand with my strange heroes
and to survey the surging immensity of life, to survey it
through the laughter that all can see and through the tears
unseen and unknown by anyone."*
— *Nikolai Gogol*

*"But man is a fickle and disreputable creature and perhaps,
like a chess-player, is interested in the process of attaining
his goal rather than the goal itself."*
— *Fyodor Dostoyevsky*

*"When a phrase is born, it is both good and bad at the
same time. The secret of its success rests in a crux
that is barely discernible. One's fingertips must grasp
the key, gently warming it. And then the key must
be turned once, not twice."*
— *Isaac Babel*

*"The longer and more carefully we look at a funny story,
the sadder it becomes."*
— *Nikolai Gogol*

*"I say let the world go to hell, but I should always
have my tea."*
— *Fyodor Dostoyevsky*

"No iron can stab the heart with such force as a period put just at the right place."
— Isaac Babel

"Two turtle doves will show thee
Where my cold ashes lie
And sadly, murmuring tell thee
How in tears I did die..."
— Nikolai Gogol

"People speak sometimes about the 'bestial' cruelty of man, but that is terribly unjust and offensive to beasts, no animal could ever be so cruel as a man, so artfully, so artistically cruel."
— Fyodor Dostoyevsky

"You're trying to live without enemies. That's all you think about, not having enemies."
— Isaac Babel

"I am who I am and that's who I am."
— Nikolai Gogol

"The second half of a man's life is made up of nothing but the habits he has acquired during the first half."
— Fyodor Dostoyevsky

"A well-thought-out story doesn't need to resemble real life. Life itself tries with all its might to resemble a well-crafted story."
— Isaac Babel

the Americans

the Americans

"Ignorance, allied with power, is the most ferocious enemy justice can have."
— James Baldwin

"What art offers is space...a certain breathing room for the spirit."
— John Updike

"You can't blame a writer for what the characters say."
— Truman Capote

"My advice to you is not to inquire why or whither, but just enjoy your ice cream while it is on your plate."
— Thornton Wilder

"Oppressive language does more than represent violence; it is violence; does more than represent the limits of knowledge; it limits knowledge."
— Toni Morrison

"To know how much there is to know is the beginning of learning to live."
— Dorothy West

"Fame means millions of people have the wrong idea of who you are."
— Erica Jong

"In summer, the song sings itself."
— William Carlos Williams

"Healing begins where the wound was made."
— Alice Walker

"Peace is always beautiful."
— Walt Whitman, **Leaves of Grass**

"To see the Summer sky, is Poetry..."
— Emily Dickinson

"I have to see a thing a thousand times before I see it once."
— Thomas Wolfe,
You Can't Go Home Again

"Curiosity killed the cat, and satisfaction brought it back."
— Eugene O'Neill

"The great thing in the world is not so much where
we stand, as in what direction we are moving."
— Oliver Wendell Holmes

"Once you have read a book you care about, some part of
it is always with you."
— Louis L'Amour

"The wounds that never heal can only be mourned alone."
— James J. Frey, **A Million Little Pieces**

Shaw, Wilder & O'Neill

Shaw, Wilder & O'Neill

"Life isn't about finding yourself. Life is about creating yourself."
— *George Bernard Shaw*

"We can only be said to be alive in those moments when our hearts are conscious of our treasures."
— *Thornton Wilder*

"The past is the present, isn't it? It's the future, too. We all try to lie out of that but life won't let us."
— *Eugene O'Neill,* **Long Day's Journey into Night**

"He knows nothing; and he thinks he knows everything. That points clearly to a political career."
— *George Bernard Shaw,* **Major Barbara**

"The highest tribute to the dead is not grief but gratitude."
— *Thornton Wilder*

"There is no present or future...only the past, happening over and over again...now."
— *Eugene O'Neill,*
A Moon for the Misbegotten

"You have learnt something. That always feels at first as if you have lost something."
— *George Bernard Shaw,* **Major Barbara**

"Oh, earth, you're too wonderful for anybody to realize you."
*— Thornton Wilder, **Our Town***

"I knew it. I knew it. Born in a hotel room — and Goddamn it — died in a hotel room."
— Eugene O'Neill

"You see things; you say, 'Why?' But I dream things that never were and I say 'Why not?'"
*— George Bernard Shaw, **Back to Methuselah***

"There is a land of the living and a land of the dead and the bridge is love, the only survival, the only meaning."
— Thornton Wilder

"We are such things as rubbish is made of, so let's drink up and forget it."
— Eugene O'Neill,
__Long Day's Journey into Night__

"The heart of an Irishman is nothing but his imagination."
— George Bernard Shaw

"If you write to impress it will always be bad, but if you write to express it will be good."
— Thornton Wilder

"You're worse than decent. You're virtuous."
— Eugene O'Neill

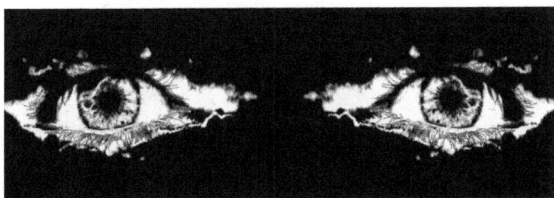

imagination

imagination

"It is rarely that the pleasures of the imagination will
compensate for the pain of sleeplessness."
— Thomas Hardy

"I am enough of an artist to draw freely upon my
imagination. Imagination is more important
than knowledge. Knowledge is limited. Imagination
encircles the world."
— Albert Einstein

"My imagination functions much better when I don't
have to speak to people."
— Patricia Highsmith

"Our imagination flies — we are its shadow on the earth."
— Vladimir Nabokov

"Imagination governs the world."
— Napoléon Bonaparte

"Reality can be beaten with enough imagination."
— Mark Twain

"Hate is a lack of imagination."
— Graham Greene

"Where there is ruin, there is hope for a treasure."
— Jalaluddin Rumi

"Imagination is the golden-eyed monster that never sleeps.
It must be fed; it cannot be ignored."
— Patricia A. McKillip

"Vision is the art of seeing things invisible."
— Jonathan Swift

"Imagination is the voice of daring. If there is anything
godlike about God, it is that. He dared to
imagine everything."
— Henry Miller, **Sexus**

"Adventure is not outside man; it is within."
— George Eliot

"To know is nothing at all; to imagine is everything."
— Anatole France

"My imagination will get me a passport to hell one day."
— John Steinbeck, **East of Eden**

"What I fear most, I think, is the death of the imagination."
— Sylvia Plath

"Some might think that the creativity, imagination, and
lights of fancy that give my life meaning are insanity."
— Vladimir Nabokov

"She is written in a foreign tongue."
— Henry James, **The Portrait of a Lady**

what is past...

what is past...

*"He who controls the past controls the future. He who
controls the present controls the past."*
— *George Orwell,* **1984**

*"Sometimes, I feel the past and the future pressing so hard
on either side that there's no room for the present at all."*
— *Evelyn Waugh,* **Brideshead Revisited**

*"When we think of the past it's the beautiful things
we pick out. We want to believe it was all like that."*
— *Margaret Atwood,* **The Handmaid's Tale**

*"What matters in life is not what happens to you
but what you remember and how you remember it."*
— *Gabriel Garcia Marquez*

*"Just remember who you are... The world will try to
change you into someone else. Don't let them.
That's the best advice anyone can give you."*
— *Cinda Williams Chima,* **The Warrior Heir**

*"The reason a writer writes a book is to forget a book
and the reason a reader reads one is to remember it."*
— *Thomas Wolfe*

"When it comes to the past, everyone writes fiction."
— *Stephen King*

"I may not always be with you
But when we're far apart
Remember you will be with me
Right inside my heart."
— Marc Wambolt, **Poems from the Heart**

"I should like to bury something precious in every place
where I've been happy and then, when I'm old and ugly
and miserable, I could come back and dig it up
and remember."
— Evelyn Waugh, **Brideshead Revisited**

"Life can only be understood backwards; but it must
be lived forwards."
— Søren Kierkegaard

"Scars have the strange power to remind us that our
past is real."
— Cormac McCarthy

"It is by no means an irrational fancy that, in a future
existence, we shall look upon what we think our present
existence, as a dream."
— Edgar Allan Poe

"No people whose word for 'yesterday' is the same as
their word for 'tomorrow' can be said to have a firm
grip on the time."
— Salman Rushdie

soldiers

soldiers

"War is sweet to those who have never fought."
— *Jess Rothenberg*

"Listen up: there's no war that will end all wars."
— *Haruki Murakami,* **Kafka on the Shore**

"The world is full enough of hurts and mischances
without wars to multiply them."
— *J.R.R. Tolkien,* **The Return of the King**

"It doesn't make a damned bit of difference who wins
the war to someone who's dead."
— *Joseph Heller,* **Catch-22**

"He who conquers himself is the mightiest warrior."
— *Confucius*

"The purpose of all war is peace."
— *St. Augustine*

"In this era of world wars, in this atomic age, values
have changed. We have learned that we are guests of
existence, travelers between two stations. We must
discover security within ourselves."
— *Boris Pasternak*

"Laws are inoperative in war."
— *Cicero*

"Never interrupt your enemy when he is making a mistake."
— *Napoléon Bonaparte*

"Nothing except a battle lost can be half as melancholy as a battle won."
— *Duke of Wellington*

"All we can know is that we know nothing. And that's the height of human wisdom."
— *Leo Tolstoy*, **War and Peace**

"Give us the future...we've had enough of your past. Give us back our country to live in — to grow in...to love."
— *Michael Collins*

"War is peace. Freedom is slavery. Ignorance is strength."
— *George Orwell*

"It's courage, not luck, that takes us through to the end of the road."
— *Ruskin Bond*

"'Life is simple,' I said. 'Ale, women, sword, and reputation. Nothing else matters.'"
— *Bernard Cornwell*,
The Pale Horseman

"For after the Battle comes quiet."
— *H.G. Wells*, **The Time Machine**

death

death

*"Though one were strong as seven,
He too with death shall dwell,
Nor wake with wings in Heaven,
Nor weep for pains in Hell."*
— *Algernon Charles Swinburne,*
The Garden of Proserpine

*"Literature is the ditch I'm going to die in. It's still
the thing I care most about."*
— *Thomas McGuane*

*"The truth is simple, you do not die from love. You only
wish you did."*
— *Erica Jong*

*"When the snows fall and the white winds blow, the
lone wolf dies but the pack survives."*
— *George R.R. Martin,* **A Game of Thrones**

*"In any man who dies, there dies with him his first snow,
his first kiss, his first fight. People do not die
but worlds die within them."*
— *Yevgeny Yevtushenko*

*"Only in Russia poetry is respected — it gets people killed.
Is there anywhere else where poetry is so common
a motive for murder?"*
— *Osip Mandelstam*

"A word aptly uttered or written cannot be cut away by an axe."
— *Nikolai Gogol,* **Dead Souls**

"What difference does it make to the dead, the orphans and the homeless, whether the mad destruction is wrought under the name of totalitarianism or in the holy name of liberty or democracy?"
— *Mahatma Gandhi*

"Love never dies a natural death. It dies because we don't know how to replenish its source. It dies of blindness and errors and betrayals. It dies of illness and wounds; it dies of weariness, of witherings, of tarnishings."
— *Anaïs Nin*

"The fear of death follows from the fear of life. A man who lives fully is prepared to die at any time."
— *Mark Twain*

"I could die for you. But I couldn't, and wouldn't, live for you."
— *Ayn Rand,* **The Fountainhead**

"Yea, all things live forever, though at times they sleep and are forgotten."
— *H. Rider Haggard*

"We who think we are about to die will laugh at anything."
— *Terry Pratchett*

Ibsen & Chekhov

Ibsen & Chekhov

"To live is to war with trolls in heart and soul.
To write is to sit in judgement on oneself."
— *Henrik Ibsen,* **Peer Gynt**

"If you are afraid of loneliness, don't marry."
— *Anton Chekhov*

"You see, the point is that the strongest man in the world
is he who stands most alone."
— *Henrik Ibsen,* **An Enemy of the People**

"What a fine weather today! Can't choose whether to
drink tea or to hang myself."
— *Anton Chekhov*

"You see, there are some people that one loves, and others
that perhaps one would rather be with."
— *Henrik Ibsen,* **A Doll's House**

"To fear love is to fear life, and those whose fear life are
already three parts dead..."
— *Anton Chekhov*

"One's life is a heavy price to pay for being born."
— *Henrik Ibsen*

"Even in Siberia there is happiness."
— *Anton Chekhov*

"It's a release to know that in spite of everything a premeditated act of courage is still possible."
— *Henrik Ibsen*, **Hedda Gabler**

"There will come a time when everybody will know why, for what purpose, there is all this suffering, and there will be no more mysteries. But now we must live..."
— *Anton Chekhov*, **The Three Sisters**

"I'll risk everything together with you."
— *Henrik Ibsen*, **A Doll's House**

"In all the universe, nothing remains permanent and unchanged but the spirit."
— *Anton Chekhov*

"Public opinion is an extremely mutable thing."
— *Henrik Ibsen*, **An Enemy of the People**

"What must human beings be, to destroy what they can never create?"
— *Anton Chekhov*

"You have never loved me. You have only thought it pleasant to be in love with me."
— *Henrik Ibsen*, **A Doll's House**

"In one night, lying with one's eyes shut, one may sometimes live through more than ten years of happiness."
— *Anton Chekhov*

truth

truth

"In a time of deceit telling the truth is a revolutionary act."
— *George Orwell*

"It is not I who am strong, it is reason, it is truth."
— *Émile Zola*

"It is not true that people stop pursuing dreams because they grow old, they grow old because they stop pursuing dreams."
— *Gabriel Garcia Marquez*

"Dreams come true. Without that possibility, nature would not incite us to have them."
— *John Updike*

"The only true paradise is paradise lost."
— *Marcel Proust*

"To stand up for truth is nothing. For truth, you must sit in jail."
— *Aleksandr Solzhenitsyn*

"The true enemy of man is generalization."
— *Czesław Miłosz*

"Best be yourself, imperial, plain, and true."
— *Robert Browning*

*"Keep true. Never be ashamed of doing right. Decide what
you think is right and stick to it."*
— *George Eliot*

*"I don't care what anybody says about me as long as
it isn't true."*
— *Truman Capote*

"Never trust anyone who has not brought a book with them."
— *Lemony Snicket*

"If you tell the truth, you don't have to remember anything."
— *Mark Twain*

"The truth is rarely pure and never simple."
— *Oscar Wilde*

"Art is the lie that enables us to realize the truth."
— *Pablo Picasso*

"Rather than love, than money, than fame, give me truth."
— *Henry David Thoreau*

*"The best way to find out if you can trust somebody is
to trust them."*
— *Ernest Hemingway*

"You can't give your heart to a wild thing."
— *Truman Capote*

time

time

"If I had a flower for every time I thought of you...I could walk through my garden forever."
— Alfred, Lord Tennyson

"Don't be sad, don't be angry, if life deceives you! Submit to your grief...your time for joy will come, believe me."
— Aleksandr Pushkin

"Success does not consist in never making mistakes but in never making the same one a second time."
— George Bernard Shaw

"When someone shows you who they are believe them; the first time."
— Maya Angelou

"These young people naturally grow up with ideas different from ours, for they are born for times when we shall no longer be here."
—Émile Zola, **Work**

"Time is the longest distance between two places."
— Tennessee Williams, **The Glass Menagerie**

"The quickest way is sometimes the longest."
— Neil Gaiman

"Time is an illusion."
— *Albert Einstein*

"Time takes it all, whether you want it to or not."
— *Stephen King,* **The Green Mile**

"As if you could kill time without injuring eternity."
— *Henry David Thoreau,* **Walden**

*"The strongest of all warriors are these two — Time
and Patience."*
— *Leo Tolstoy,* **War and Peace**

*"The memory of everything is very soon overwhelmed
in time."*
— *Marcus Aurelius*

*"An infinity of passion can be contained in one minute,
like a crowd in a small space."*
— *Gustave Flaubert,* **Madame Bovary**

"Every moment has its pleasures and its hope."
— *Jane Austen,* **Mansfield Park**

*"He was sounding the deeps of his nature, and of the parts
of his nature that were deeper than he, going back into
the womb of Time."*
— *Jack London,* **The Call of the Wild**

imagine...

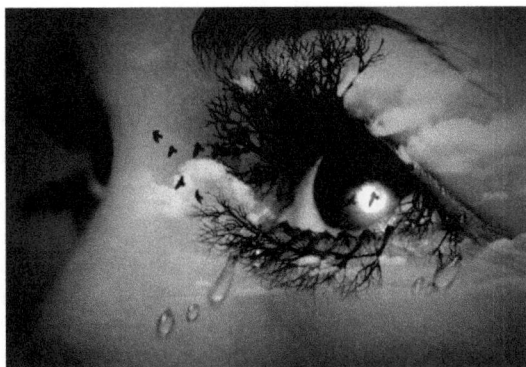

imagine...

"Yes: I am a dreamer. For a dreamer is one who can only
find his way by moonlight, and his punishment is that
he sees the dawn before the rest of the world."
— *Oscar Wilde,* **The Critic as Artist**

"Everything you can imagine is real."
— *Pablo Picasso*

"Logic will get you from A to Z; imagination will get
you everywhere."
— *Albert Einstein*

"You can't depend on your eyes when your imagination
is out of focus."
— *Mark Twain,*
A Connecticut Yankee in King Arthur's Court

"The moment you doubt whether you can fly, you cease
for ever to be able to do it."
— *J.M. Barrie,* **Peter Pan**

"A well-composed book is a magic carpet on which we
are wafted to a world that we cannot enter in any other way."
— *Caroline Gordon*

"Imagination is everything. It is the preview of life's coming
attractions."
— *Albert Einstein*

"Every great advance in science has issued from a new audacity of imagination."
— *John Dewey*

"The basis of action is lack of imagination. It is the last resource of those who know not how to dream."
— *Oscar Wilde*

"Imagination is more important than knowledge. For knowledge is limited to all we know and understand, while imagination embraces the entire world, and all there ever will be to know and understand."
— *Michael Scott,* **The Warlock**

"Every generation imagines itself to be more intelligent than the one that went before it, and wiser than the one that comes after it."
— *George Orwell*

"I don't imagine you will dispute the fact that at present the stupid people are in an absolutely overwhelming majority all the world over."
— *Henrik Ibsen*

"I am certain of nothing but the holiness of the Heart's affections and the truth of the Imagination."
— *John Keats*

"We are such stuff as dreams are made of..."
— *William Shakespeare*

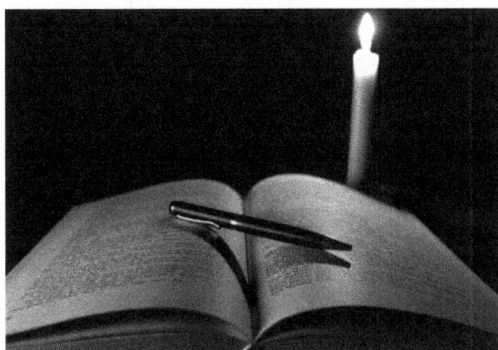

confession

confession

"The really dangerous people believe they are doing whatever they are doing solely and only because it is without question the right thing to do. And that is what makes them dangerous."
— *Neil Gaiman*

"I would always rather be happy than dignified."
— *Charlotte Brontë,* **Jane Eyre**

"My life is a perfect graveyard of buried hopes."
— *L.M. Montgomery,* **Anne of Green Gables**

"We who are beyond the mortal world see many things from the edges; we hear the subtle shifts of rhythm in the beat of a blackening heart."
— *Emmanuelle de Maupassant*

"Dull people filled him with terror."
— *Thomas Wolfe,* **Look Homeward, Angel**

"Don't wait to be hunted to hide, that was always my motto."
— *Samuel Beckett,* **Molloy**

"I read hungrily and delightedly, and have realized since that you can't write unless you read."
— *William Trevor*

"Home is where you feel at home. I'm still looking."
*— Truman Capote, **Breakfast at Tiffany's***

"Right or wrong, it's very pleasant to break something from time to time."
— Fyodor Dostoyevsky

"I must lose myself in action, lest I wither in despair."
— Alfred, Lord Tennyson

"In the next world, I could not be worse than I am in this."
— Patrick Branwell Brontë

"My mistakes are my life."
— Samuel Beckett

"I never had any doubts about my abilities. I knew I could write. I just had to figure out how to eat while doing this."
— Cormac McCarthy

"I'm yours forever, forever, and ever. Here I stand; I'm as firm as a rock. If you'll only trust me, how little you'll be disappointed. Be mine as I am yours."
*— Henry James, **The Portrait of a Lady***

"The trick is not how much pain you feel — but how much joy you feel. Any idiot can feel pain. Life is full of excuses to feel pain, excuses not to live, excuses, excuses, excuses."
— Erica Jong

Chekhov & Tolstoy

Chekhov & Tolstoy

"The role of the artist is to ask questions, not answer them."
— Anton Chekhov

*"Everyone thinks of changing the world, but no one
thinks of changing himself."*
— Leo Tolstoy

*"I must run away, I must escape this very day or I shall go
out of my mind."*
— Anton Chekhov

*"He stepped down, trying not to look long at her, as if she
were the sun, yet he saw her, like the sun, even
without looking."*
— Leo Tolstoy, **Anna Karenina**

*"We just philosophize, complain of boredom, or drink vodka.
It's so clear, you see, that if we're to begin living in the
present, we must first of all redeem our past and then
be done with it forever."*
— Anton Chekhov, **The Cherry Orchard**

*"All happy families are alike; each unhappy family is
unhappy in its own way."*
— Leo Tolstoy, **Anna Karenina**

"We shall find peace. We shall hear angels, we shall see the sky sparkling with diamonds."
— *Anton Chekhov*

"It is amazing how complete is the delusion that beauty is goodness."
— *Leo Tolstoy,* **The Kreutzer Sonata**

"Wisdom....comes not from age, but from education and learning."
— *Anton Chekhov*

"Rummaging in our souls, we often dig up something that ought to have lain there unnoticed."
— *Leo Tolstoy,* **Anna Karenina**

"If my life can ever be of any use to you, come and take it."
— *Anton Chekhov,* **The Seagull**

"Respect was invented to cover the empty place where love should be."
— *Leo Tolstoy,* **Anna Karenina**

"Man, is what he believes."
— *Anton Chekhov*

"If you look for perfection, you'll never be content."
— *Leo Tolstoy,* **Anna Karenina**

politics

politics

"There are no facts, only interpretations."
— *Friedrich Nietzsche*

"The simple step of a courageous individual is not to take part in the lie. One word of truth outweighs the world."
— *Aleksandr Solzhenitsyn*

"Those who cannot change their minds cannot change anything."
— *George Bernard Shaw*

"Integrity without knowledge is weak and useless, and knowledge without integrity is dangerous and dreadful."
— *Samuel Johnson*

"Reader, suppose you were an idiot. And suppose you were a member of Congress. But I repeat myself."
— *Mark Twain*

"All thinking men are atheists."
— *Ernest Hemingway,* **A Farewell to Arms**

"I was not born to amuse the Tsars."
— *Aleksandr Pushkin*

"In politics, stupidity is not a handicap."
— *Napoléon Bonaparte*

"Politics in a literary work, is like a gun shot in the middle
of a concert, something vulgar, and however, something
which is impossible to ignore."
— Stendhal

"Loyalty to country ALWAYS. Loyalty to government,
when it deserves it."
— Mark Twain

"Patriotism is the last refuge of a scoundrel."
— Samuel Johnson

"Patriotism is, fundamentally, a conviction that a particular
country is the best in the world because you were
born in it...."
— George Bernard Shaw

"And if you ask again whether there is any justice in the
world, you'll have to be satisfied with the reply: not for the
time being; at any rate, not up to this Friday."
— Alfred Doblin

"If you do not tell the truth about yourself you cannot
tell it about other people."
— Virginia Woolf

"The difference between a rebel and a patriot depends
upon who is in power at the moment."
— Sidney Sheldon, **Sands of Time**

truths

truths

"It's better to look at the sky than live there. Such an empty
place; so vague. Just a country where the thunder goes."
— *Truman Capote*, **Breakfast at Tiffany's**

"Think you're escaping and run into yourself. Longest way
round is the shortest way home."
— *James Joyce*, **Ulysses**

"It takes something more than intelligence to act
intelligently."
— *Fyodor Dostoyevsky*, **Crime and Punishment**

"There are books of which the backs and covers are by far
the best parts."
— *Charles Dickens*, **Oliver Twist**

"And what is laughter anyway? Changing the angle
of vision."
— *Erica Jong*, **Fear of Fifty**

"It is better to suffer wrong than to do it, and happier
to be sometimes cheated than not to trust."
— *Samuel Johnson*

"There is no exercise better for the heart than reaching down
and lifting people up."
— *John Holmes*

"A good enemy can be better than the best of friend."
— Simona Panova

"The greater the obstacle, the more glory in overcoming it."
— Molière

"Art is a corner of creation seen through a temperament."
— Émile Zola

*"No one is useless in this world who lightens the burdens
of another."*
— Charles Dickens

"Oft hope is born when all is forlorn."
— J.R.R. Tolkien, **The Return of the King**

"You're on Earth. There's no cure for that."
— Samuel Beckett

*"The worst thing about jealousy is how low it makes
you reach."*
— Erica Jong, **How to Save Your Own Life**

"Our envy of others devours us most of all."
— Aleksandr Solzhenitsyn

*"When you have a sorrow that is too great it leaves no
room for any other."*
— Émile Zola

life & hope

life & hope

"*Life has no plot. It is by far more interesting than anything you can say about it...*"
— *Erica Jong,* **Fear of Flying**

"*She wondered that hope was so much harder than despair.*"
— *Patricia Briggs,* **Cry Wolf**

"*This is love: to fly toward a secret sky, to cause a hundred veils to fall each moment. First to let go of life. Finally, to take a step without feet.*"
— *Jalaluddin Rumi*

"*To be truly radical is to make hope possible rather than despair convincing.*"
— *Raymond Williams*

"*Life seems to go on without effort when I am filled with music.*"
— *George Eliot,* **The Mill on the Floss**

"*It is necessary to hope...for hope itself is happiness.*"
— *Samuel Johnson*

"*He did not care if she was heartless, vicious and vulgar, stupid and grasping, he loved her. He would rather have misery with one than happiness with the other.*"
— *W. Somerset Maugham,* **Of Human Bondage**

"The difference between hope and despair is a different way of telling stories from the same facts."
— Alain de Botton

"I have lived my life according to this principle: if I'm afraid of it, then I must do it."
— Erica Jong

"Being a cheerful hobbit, he had not needed hope, as long as despair, could be postponed."
— J.R.R. Tolkien,
The Two Towers

"There are darknesses in life and there are lights, and you are one of the lights, the light of all lights."
— Bram Stoker, **Dracula**

*"I loved you silently, without hope, fully,
In diffidence, in jealousy, in pain;
I loved you so tenderly and truly,
As let you else be loved by any man."*
— Aleksandr Pushkin

"We must leave our mark on life while we have it in our power."
— Karen Blixen

"Be regular and orderly in your life, so that you may be violent and original in your work."
— Gustave Flaubert

friends

friends

"The best mirror is an old friend."
— George Herbert

"The capacity for friendship is God's way of apologizing for our families."
*— Jay McInerney, **The Last of the Savages***

"Friendship marks a life even more deeply than love. Love risks degenerating into obsession, friendship is never anything but sharing."
— Elie Wiesel

"Books are the quietest and most constant of friends; they are the most accessible and wisest of counselors, and the most patient of teachers."
— Charles William Eliot

"Animals are such agreeable friends — they ask no questions, they pass no criticisms."
*— George Eliot, **Mr. Gilfil's Love Story***

"There is nothing I would not do for those who are really my friends. I have no notion of loving people by halves, it is not my nature."
*— Jane Austen, **Northanger Abbey***

"Friendship...is born at the moment when one man says to another 'What! You too? I thought that no one but myself...'"
— C.S. Lewis, **The Four Loves**

"You can't stay in your corner of the Forest waiting for others to come to you. You have to go to them sometimes."
— A.A. Milne, **Winnie-the-Pooh**

"What is a friend? A single soul dwelling in two bodies."
— Aristotle

"I am glad you are here with me. Here at the end of all things, Sam."
— J.R.R. Tolkien,
The Return of the King

"I got you to look after me, and you got me to look after you, and that's why."
— John Steinbeck, **Of Mice and Men**

"Wishing to be friends is quick work, but friendship is a slow ripening fruit."
— Aristotle

"If you have two friends in your lifetime, you're lucky. If you have one good friend, you're more than lucky."
— S.E. Hinton

the Victorians

the Victorians

"I show you doubt, to prove that faith exists."
— Robert Browning

*"One must have a heart of stone to read the death of
little Nell without laughing."*
— Oscar Wilde

*"But injustice breeds injustice; the fighting with shadows
and being defeated by them necessitates the setting up
of substances to combat."*
— Charles Dickens, **Bleak House**

*"Though sympathy alone can't alter facts, it can help to make
them more bearable."*
— Bram Stoker, **Dracula**

"It is always fatal to have music or poetry interrupted."
— George Eliot, **Middlemarch**

*"Ah, but a man's reach should exceed his grasp,
Or what's a heaven for?"*
— Robert Browning

*"An artist should create beautiful things, but should put
nothing of his own life into them."*
— Oscar Wilde

"There are very few moments in a man's existence when he experiences so much ludicrous distress, or meets with so little charitable commiseration, as when he is in pursuit of his own hat."
— *Charles Dickens,* **The Pickwick Papers**

"Loneliness will sit over our roofs with brooding wings."
— *Bram Stoker,* **Dracula**

"People are almost always better than their neighbors think they are."
— *George Eliot,* **Middlemarch**

"Grow old along with me! The best is yet to be, the last of life, for which the first was made. Our times are in his hand who saith, 'A whole I planned, youth shows but half; Trust God: See all, nor be afraid!'"
— *Robert Browning*

"Those who find beautiful meanings in beautiful things are the cultivated. For these there is hope...."
— *Oscar Wilde*

"You have been the last dream of my soul."
— *Charles Dickens,* **A Tale of Two Cities**

"What do we live for, if it is not to make life less difficult for each other?"
— *George Eliot*

winter

winter

"If winter comes, can spring be far behind?"
— *Percy Bysshe Shelley*, **Ode to the West Wind**

"I think it was Milosz, the Polish poet, who when he lay
in a doorway and watched the bullets lifting the cobbles
out of the street beside him realized that most poetry is
not equipped for life in a world where people actually die..."
— *Ted Hughes*, **Winter Pollen: Occasional Prose**

"For they are the knights of summer, and winter is coming."
— *George R.R. Martin*, **A Game of Thrones**

"What good is the warmth of summer, without the cold
of winter to give it sweetness."
— *John Steinbeck*

"Winter is not a season, it's an occupation."
— *Sinclair Lewis*

"There's a certain Slant of light,
Winter Afternoons..."
— *Emily Dickinson*

"Laughter is the sun that drives winter from the
human face."
— *Victor Hugo*

"A sad tale's best for winter..."
— William Shakespeare

"In this world, only winter is certain."
— George R.R. Martin, **A Dance with Dragons**

*"Isn't it true that a pleasant house makes winter
more poetic..."*
— Charles Baudelaire

*"In the bleak mid-winter
Frosty wind made moan,
Earth stood hard as iron,
Water like a stone..."*
— Christina Rossetti

*"A winter Eden in an alder swamp
Where conies now come out to sun and romp,
As near a paradise as it can be..."*
— Robert Frost

*"And in winter, under my greatcoat, I wrapped myself
in swathes of newspaper, and did not shed them until
the earth awoke, for good, in April..."*
— Samuel Beckett

*"You think of outside your room, of the streets of the town,
the lonely little squares over by the station, of those winter
Saturdays all alike."*
— Marguerite Duras, **The Malady of Death**

women

women

"A word after a word after a word is power."
— *Margaret Atwood*

"My mission in life is not merely to survive, but to thrive; and to do so with some passion, some compassion, some humor, and some style."
— *Maya Angelou*

"Winter is the time for comfort, for good food and warmth, for the touch of a friendly hand and for a talk beside the fire..."
— *Edith Sitwell*

"If I read a book and it makes my whole body so cold no fire can ever warm me, I know that is poetry."
— *Emily Dickinson*

"I have only to break into the tightness of a strawberry, and I see summer — its dust and lowering skies."
— *Toni Morrison*

"Beware; for I am fearless, and therefore powerful."
— *Mary Shelley,* **Frankenstein**

"We can't behave like people in novels, though, can we?"
— *Edith Wharton,* **The Age of Innocence**

"When I am grown up I shall carry a notebook — a fat book with many pages, methodically lettered. I shall enter my phrases."
— *Virginia Woolf,* **The Waves**

"...I am with fire between my teeth and still nothing but my blank page."
— *Monique Wittig*

"Writers are a superior breed. No one else can face so much rejection and still thrive."
— *Susie Smith*

"And, of course men know best about everything, except what women know better."
— *George Eliot,* **Middlemarch**

"The past is never where you think you left it."
— *Katherine Anne Porter*

"I would rather walk with a friend in the dark, than alone in the light."
— *Helen Keller*

"We should meet in another life, we should meet in air, me and you."
— *Sylvia Plath*

"Terror made me cruel..."
— *Emily Brontë,* **Wuthering Heights**

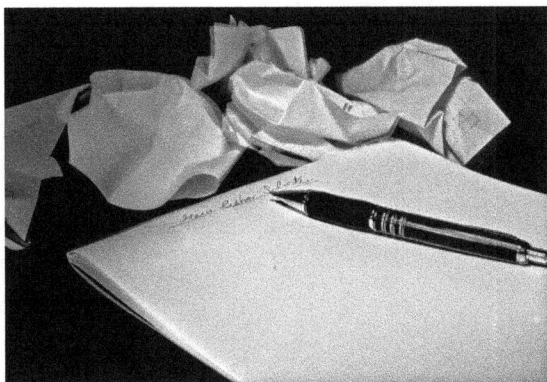

writing...

writing...

"Don't tell me the moon is shining; show me light glinting on broken glass."
— Henrik Ibsen

"There is no greater agony than bearing an untold story inside you."
— Maya Angelou

"The question is not what you look at, but what you see."
— Robert Frost

"Use all this life to make yourself a great writer, thoughtful and kind, slowly, surely over the years."
— T.K. Naliaka

"I have never believed in the axiom that a writer should first and foremost, write about what he knows. I think it's a piece of misinformation."
— William Trevor

"Obstacles are those frightening things you see when you take your eyes off your goal."
— Henry James

"If you ask me what I came to do in this world, I, an artist, will answer you: I am here to live out loud."
— Émile Zola

"Anyone who ever gave you confidence, you owe them a lot."
— *Truman Capote,* **Breakfast at Tiffany's**

"The first thing you have to learn when you go into the arts
is to learn to cope with rejection.
If you can't, you're dead."
— *Warren Adler*

"I write what I want to read. If I were to write what I
know, I'd be staring at a blank page forever."
— *R.J. Dennis*

"The great artists of the world are never Puritans,
and seldom even ordinarily respectable."
— *H.L. Mencken*

"Every production of an artist should be the expression of
an adventure of his soul."
— *W. Somerset Maugham,* **The Summing Up**

"I am irritated by my own writing. I am like a violinist
whose ear is true, but whose fingers refuse to reproduce
precisely the sound he hears within."
— *Gustave Flaubert*

"To be a poet is a condition, not a profession."
— *Robert Frost*

"Try to be one of those on whom nothing is lost."
— *Henry James,* **The Art of Fiction**

always reading...

always reading...

*"It is what you read when you don't have to that determines
what you will be when you can't help it."*
— *Oscar Wilde*

"Books are a uniquely portable magic."
— *Stephen King,*
On Writing: A Memoir of the Craft

*"I can survive well enough on my own — if given the proper
reading material."*
— *Sarah J. Maas,* **Throne of Glass**

*"Everything in the world exists in order to end up
as a book."*
— *Stéphane Mallarmé*

*"Reading was my escape and my comfort, my consolation,
my stimulant of choice: reading for the pure pleasure
of it, for the beautiful stillness that surrounds you when
you hear an author's words reverberating in your head."*
— *Paul Auster,*
The Brooklyn Follies

*"The worst thing about new books is that they keep
us from reading the old ones."*
— *Joseph Joubert*

"Reading is the sole means by which we slip, involuntarily, often helplessly, into another's skin, another's voice, another's soul."
— Joyce Carol Oates

"There is no friend as loyal as a book."
— Ernest Hemingway

"A writer only begins a book. A reader finishes it."
— Samuel Johnson

"A book burrows into your life in a very profound way because the experience of reading is not passive."
— Erica Jong

"Reading is like thinking, like praying, like talking to a friend, like expressing your ideas, like listening to other people's ideas, like listening to music, like looking at the view, like taking a walk on the beach."
— Roberto Bolaño, **2666**

"To acquire the habit of reading is to construct for yourself a refuge from almost all the miseries of life."
— W. Somerset Maugham, **Books and You**

"Any book that helps a child to form a habit of reading, to make reading one of his deep and continuing needs, is good for him."
— Maya Angelou

Landtſperg.

the Germans

the Germans

*"Deeper meaning resides in the fairy tales told me in
my childhood than any truth that is taught in life."*
— *Friedrich Schiller*

*"But the main things about a man are his eyes and his feet.
He should be able to see the world and go after it."*
— *Alfred Doblin*

*"It isn't easy to accept that suffering can also be beautiful...
It's difficult. It's something you can only understand
if you dig deeply into yourself."*
— *Rainer Werner Fassbinder*

*"The human race tends to remember the abuses to which
it has been subjected rather than the endearments. What's
left of kisses? Wounds, however, leave scars."*
— *Bertolt Brecht*

"A harmful truth is better than a useful lie."
— *Thomas Mann,* **The Magic Mountain**

"Learn what is to be taken seriously and laugh at the rest."
— *Hermann Hesse*

*"Daring ideas are like chessmen moved forward. They may be
beaten, but they may start a winning game."*
— *Johann Wolfgang von Goethe*

"Who reflects too much will accomplish little."
— Friedrich Schiller

"Such is life: the silliest of proverbs prove to be true, and when a man thinks, now it's all right, it's not all right by a longshot."
— Alfred Doblin

"For all of us it's the things that won't work that keep our interest."
— Rainer Werner Fassbinder

"Art is not a mirror held up to reality but a hammer with which to shape it."
— Bertolt Brecht

"In books, we never find anything but ourselves. Strangely enough, that always gives us great pleasure, and we say the author is a genius."
— Thomas Mann

"Whoever wants music instead of noise, joy instead of pleasure, soul instead of gold, creative work instead of business, passion instead of foolery, finds no home in this trivial world of ours."
— Hermann Hesse

"A man sees in the world what he carries in his heart."
— Johann Wolfgang von Goethe, **Faust**

words...

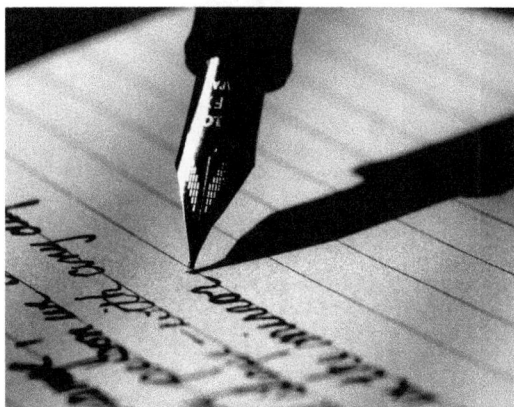

words...

"All human wisdom is contained in these two words:
Wait and Hope."
— Alexandre Dumas,
The Count of Monte Cristo

"This is one of the disadvantages of wine, it makes
a man mistake words for thoughts."
— Samuel Johnson

"I think that hate is a feeling that can only exist where
there is no understanding."
— Tennessee Williams, **Sweet Bird of Youth**

"One ought, every day at least, to hear a little song,
read a good poem, see a fine picture, and, if it were
possible, to speak a few reasonable words."
— Johann Wolfgang von Goethe,
Wilhelm Meister's Apprenticeship

"For last year's words belong to last year's language
And next year's words await another voice."
— T.S. Eliot, **Four Quartets**

"We always see our worst selves. Our most vulnerable
selves. We need someone else to get close enough
to tell us we're wrong. Someone we trust."
— David Levithan

"Every word is like an unnecessary stain on silence and nothingness."
— Samuel Beckett

"A word in earnest is as good as a speech."
*— Charles Dickens, **Bleak House***

"I hold any writer sufficiently justified who is himself in love with his theme."
— Henry James

"In a room where
people unanimously maintain
a conspiracy of silence,
one word of truth
sounds like a pistol shot."
— Czesław Miłosz

"Poetry is when an emotion has found its thought and the thought has found words."
— Robert Frost

"I've learned that people will forget what you said, people will forget what you did, but people will never forget how you made them feel."
— Maya Angelou

"A classic is a book that has never finished saying what it has to say."
— Italo Calvino

the poets

the poets

"Music was my refuge. I could crawl into the space between the notes and curl my back to loneliness."
— *Maya Angelou*

"If I can stop one heart from breaking, I shall not live in vain."
— *Emily Dickinson*

"A poem begins as a lump in the throat, a sense of wrong, a homesickness, a lovesickness."
— *Robert Frost*

"Critics write out of intellectual exercise, not poets. Poets write straight from the heart."
— *Erica Jong*

"The purpose of poetry is to remind us how difficult it is to remain just one person..."
— *Czesław Miłosz*

"Every heart sings a song, incomplete, until another heart whispers back. Those who wish to sing always find a song. At the touch of a lover, everyone becomes a poet."
— *Plato*

"Human nature is like water: it takes the shape of its container."
— *Wallace Stevens*

"I was made and meant to look for you and wait for you
and become yours forever."
— Robert Browning

"There is not a particle of life which does not bear poetry
within it."
— Gustave Flaubert

"Poetry and art are the breath of life to her."
— Edith Wharton, **The Age of Innocence**

"To do the useful thing, to say the courageous thing,
to contemplate the beautiful thing: that is enough
for one man's life."
— T.S. Eliot

"Years steal fire from the mind as vigor from the limb;
and life's enchanted cup but sparkles near the brim."
— George Gordon, Lord Byron

"It is difficult to write a paradiso when all the superficial
indications are that you ought to write an apocalypse."
— Ezra Pound

"Happiness, not in another place but this place...not for
another hour, but this hour."
— Walt Whitman

"Love is so short, forgetting is so long."
— Pablo Neruda, **Love: Ten Poems**

the dramatists

the dramatists

"You use a glass mirror to see your face; you use works of art to see your soul."
— *George Bernard Shaw*, **Back to Methuselah**

"The art of our necessities is strange
That can make vile things precious."
— *William Shakespeare*, **King Lear**

"If one wants to lead a good life, A HUMAN LIFE,
one must work."
— *Anton Chekhov*

"I suppose I have found it easier to identify with the characters
who verge upon hysteria, who were frightened of life, who were
desperate to reach out to another person. But these seemingly
fragile people are the strong people really."
— *Tennessee Williams*

"To be able to write a play, a man must be sensitive,
imaginative, naive, gullible, passionate; he must be
something of an imbecile, something of a poet,
something of a liar, something of a damned fool."
— *Robert E. Sherwood*

"If you have no wounds, how can you know if
you're alive?"
— *Edward Albee*

"I have loved him too much not to hate."
*— Jean Racine, **Andromaque***

"One ought to examine himself for a very long time before thinking of condemning others."
— Molière

"It's very difficult to feel contempt for others when you see yourself in the mirror."
— Harold Pinter

"A man must dream a long time in order to act with grandeur, and dreaming is nursed in darkness."
— Jean Genet

"I'll never waste my dreams by falling asleep. Never again."
*— Eugène Ionesco, **Man with Bags***

"Mirrors should think longer before they reflect."
— Jean Cocteau

"Life is a shipwreck, but we must not forget to sing in the lifeboats."
— Voltaire

"A play is fiction — and fiction is fact distilled into truth."
— Edward Albee

life & love

life & love

*"There is only one happiness in this life, to love and
be loved."*
— *George Sand*

*"It is a wonderful seasoning of all enjoyments to think of
those we love."*
— *Molière*

*"I did not know it was possible to be so miserable and
live but I am told that this is a common experience."*
— *Evelyn Waugh*

*"If you love me as you say you do, make it so that I am
at peace."*
— *Leo Tolstoy,* **Anna Karenina**

"Always try to keep a patch of sky above your life."
— *Marcel Proust,* **Swann's Way**

*"The great tragedy of life is not that men perish, but that
they cease to love."*
— *W. Somerset Maugham*

"Man is born to live, not to prepare for life."
— *Boris Pasternak*

"Love is the energy of life."
— *Robert Browning*

"Let yourself be drawn by the stronger pull of that which you truly love."
— *Jalaluddin Rumi*

"She wanted to die, but she also wanted to live in Paris."
— *Gustave Flaubert,* **Madame Bovary**

"There are no faster or firmer friendships than those formed between people who love the same books."
— *Irving Stone*

"I have accepted fear as part of life — specifically the fear of change...I have gone ahead despite the pounding in the heart that says: turn back...."
— *Erica Jong*

"I believe a strong woman may be stronger than a man, particularly if she happens to have love in her heart. I guess a loving woman is indestructible."
— *John Steinbeck,* **East of Eden**

"We're all sentenced to solitary confinement inside our own skins, for life."
— *Tennessee Williams*

"Love will find a way through paths where wolves fear to prey."
— *George Gordon, Lord Byron*

"Life is always either a tightrope or a feather bed. Give me the tightrope."
— *Edith Wharton*

writers

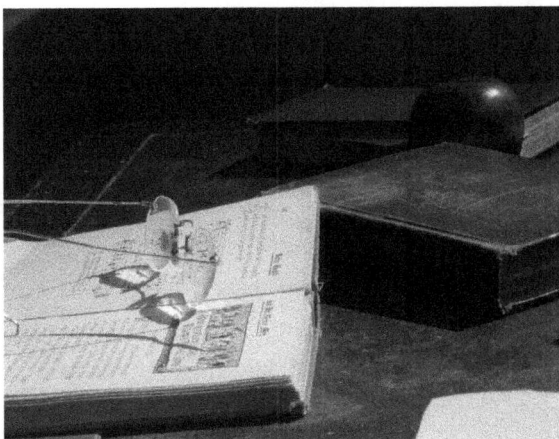

writers

"Good writers define reality; bad ones merely restate it.
A good writer turns fact into truth; a bad writer will,
more often than not, accomplish the opposite."
— *Edward Albee*

"In America, the race goes to the loud, the solemn, the
hustler. If you think you're a great writer,
you must say that you are."
— *Gore Vidal*

"When a writer is born into a family, the family
is finished."
— *Czesław Miłosz*

"A writer who is afraid to overreach himself is as useless
as a general who is afraid to be wrong."
— *Raymond Chandler*, **Pearls are a Nuisance**

"I'm writing. The pages are starting to stack up. My
morale is improving the more I feel like a writer."
— *Neil Gaiman*

"I never desire to converse with a man who has written
more than he has read."
— *Samuel Johnson*

"Good writing excites me, and makes life worth living."
— *Harold Pinter*

*"If any wish to write in a clear style, let him be first clear
in his thoughts; and if any would write in a noble
style, let him first possess a noble soul."*
— Johann Wolfgang von Goethe

*"Nothing quite has reality for me till I write it all down,
revising and embellishing as I go. I'm always waiting
for things to be over so I can get home and commit
them to paper."*
— Erica Jong

*"There are no rules of architecture for a castle in
the clouds."*
— G.K. Chesterton

*"And what, you ask, does writing teach us? First and
foremost, it reminds us that we are alive and that it is
a gift and a privilege, not a right."*
— Ray Bradbury, **Zen in the Art of Writing**

*"Respond to every call
that excites your spirit."*
— Jalaluddin Rumi, **The Essential Rumi**

*"Doubt...is an illness that comes from knowledge and leads
to madness."*
— Gustave Flaubert, **Memoirs of a Madman**

*"A writer is someone for whom writing is more difficult
than it is for other people."*
— Thomas Mann, **Essays of Three Decades**

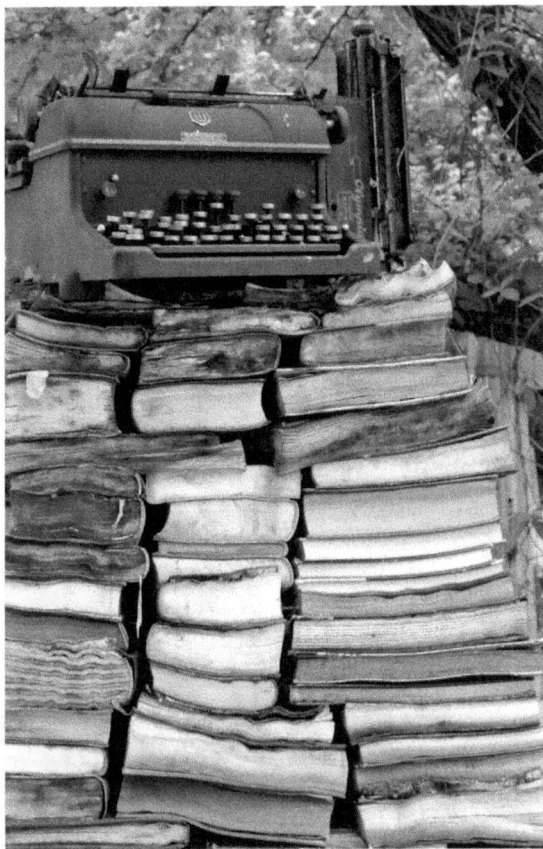

the novelists

the novelists

*"Happiness is like those palaces in fairytales whose gates
are guarded by dragons: we must fight in order to
conquer it."*
— Alexandre Dumas

*"I used to think great teachers inspire you. Now I think
I had it wrong. Good teachers inspire you; great teachers
show you how to inspire yourself every day of your life."*
— Alfred Doblin

*"It's you who are telling me; opening my eyes to things I'd
looked at so long that I'd ceased to see them."*
— Edith Wharton

*"We do not have to visit a madhouse to find disordered
minds; our planet is the mental institution of the universe."*
— Johann Wolfgang von Goethe

*"This was love at first sight, love everlasting: a feeling
unknown, unhoped for, unexpected...in so far as it could be
a matter of conscious awareness; it took entire possession
of him, and he understood, with joyous amazement,
that this was for life."*
— Thomas Mann

"I guess there are never enough books."
— John Steinbeck

"There is no such thing as chance; and what seems to us merest accident springs from the deepest source of destiny."
— *Friedrich Schiller*

"How many a man has dated a new era in his life from the reading of a book."
— *Henry David Thoreau,* **Walden**

"One can acquire everything in solitude except character."
— *Stendhal*

"Nothing is so necessary for a young man as the company of intelligent women."
— *Leo Tolstoy,* **War and Peace**

"Don't let us forget that the causes of human actions are usually immeasurably more complex and varied than our subsequent explanations of them."
— *Fyodor Dostoyevsky,* **The Idiot**

"Do you want me to tell you something really subversive? Love is everything it's cracked up to be. That's why people are so cynical about it. It really is worth fighting for, being brave for, risking everything for. And the trouble is, if you don't risk anything, you risk even more."
— *Erica Jong,* **Fear of Flying**

"I want you to believe...to believe in things that you cannot."
— *Bram Stoker,* **Dracula**

desire

desire

"I desired dragons with a profound desire."
— *C.S. Lewis*

"I've lived to bury my desires,
And see my dreams corrode with rust;
Now all that's left are fruitless fires
That burn my empty heart to dust."
— *Aleksandr Pushkin*

"There is a candle in your heart, ready to be kindled.
There is a void in your soul, ready to be filled.
You feel it, don't you?"
— *Jalaluddin Rumi*

"Boredom: the desire for desires."
— *Leo Tolstoy*

"The desire to reach for the stars is ambitious. The desire to
reach hearts is wise."
— *Maya Angelou*

"I don't want realism. I want magic!"
— *Tennessee Williams*,
A Streetcar Named Desire

"Sin ought to be something exquisite, my dear boy."
— *Émile Zola*

"Worse than not realizing the dreams of your youth would be to have been young and never dreamed at all."
— Jean Genet

"How sad and bad and mad it was...but then, how it was sweet..."
— Robert Browning

"I would like to be the air that inhabits you for a moment only. I would like to be that unnoticed and that necessary."
— Margaret Atwood

"We love the things we love for what they are."
— Robert Frost

"How wonderful to be alive, he thought. But why does it always hurt?"
— Boris Pasternak, **Doctor Zhivago**

"I have not broken your heart — you have broken it; and in breaking it, you have broken mine."
— Emily Brontë, **Wuthering Heights**

"I love her beauty, but I fear her mind."
— Stendhal

"That man is the richest whose pleasures are the cheapest."
— Henry David Thoreau

American poets

American poets

"That it will never come again is what makes life so sweet."
— Emily Dickinson

"This is the way the world ends
Not with a bang but a whimper."
— T.S. Eliot

"In three words, I can sum up everything I've learned about
life: it goes on."
— Robert Frost

"Have enough courage to trust love one more time and
always one more time."
— Maya Angelou

"There is no Frigate like a Book
To take us Lands away
Nor any Coursers like a Page
Of prancing Poetry..."
— Emily Dickinson

"The very existence of libraries affords the best evidence
that we may yet have hope for the future of man."
— T.S. Eliot

"Freedom lies in being bold."
— Robert Frost

*"You may not control all the events that happen to you,
but you can decide not to be reduced by them."*
— *Maya Angelou*

"One need not be a chamber to be haunted."
— *Emily Dickinson,* **The Complete Poems**

"I will show you fear in a handful of dust."
— *T.S. Eliot*

"Happiness makes up in height for what it lacks in length."
— *Robert Frost*

*"Success is liking yourself, liking what you do, and liking
how you do it."*
— *Maya Angelou*

"Dying is a wild night and a new road."
— *Emily Dickinson*

"Genuine poetry can communicate before it is understood."
— *T.S. Eliot*

*"How many things would you attempt
If you knew you could not fail?"*
— *Robert Frost*

*"I did then what I knew how to do. Now that I know
better, I do better."*
— *Maya Angelou*

books...

books...

"I kept always two books in my pocket, one to read,
one to write in."
— *Robert Louis Stevenson*

"The best books...are those that tell you what you
know already."
— *George Orwell,* **1984**

"I want to write books that unlock the traffic jam
in everybody's head."
— *John Updike*

"A novel is a mirror walking along a main road."
— *Stendhal,* **The Red and the Black**

"Books must be read as deliberately and reservedly as they
were written."
— *Henry David Thoreau,* **Walden**

"He never went out without a book under his arm, and he
often came back with two."
— *Victor Hugo,* **Les Misérables**

"The only important thing in a book is the meaning that it
has for you."
— *W. Somerset Maugham*

"No book can ever be finished. While working on it we learn just enough to find it immature the moment we turn away from it."
— *Karl R. Popper*

"I stand in the mist and cry, thinking of myself standing in the mist and crying, and wondering if I will ever be able to use this experience in a book."
— *Erica Jong,* **Fear of Flying**

"A good book has no ending."
— *Robert Frost*

"Ladies know what to guard against, because they read novels that tell them of these tricks..."
— *Thomas Hardy,*
Tess of the D'Urbervilles

"What is written without effort is in general read without pleasure."
— *Samuel Johnson*

"If I could always read I should never feel the want of company."
— *George Gordon, Lord Byron*

"I read like the flame reads the wood."
— *Alfred Doblin*

the French

the French

"When you compare the sorrows of real life to the pleasures
of the imaginary one, you will never want to live again,
only to dream forever."
— *Alexandre Dumas*,
The Count of Monte Cristo

"When there is no hope in the future, the present appears
atrociously bitter."
— *Émile Zola*

"To love or have loved, that is enough. Ask nothing further.
There is no other pearl to be found in the dark folds of life."
— *Victor Hugo*, **Les Misérables**

"If you don't love me, it does not matter, anyway I can love
for the both of us."
— *Stendhal*

"The more we love someone, the less we flatter them;
it is by excusing nothing that true love shows itself."
— *Molière*

"Every man is guilty of all the good he did not do."
— *Voltaire*

"The more one judges, the less one loves."
— *Honoré de Balzac*

"Man is always prey to his truths. Once he has admitted
them, he cannot free himself from them."
— Albert Camus

"It comes so soon, the moment when there is nothing
left to wait for."
— Marcel Proust

"One can be the master of what one does, but never of
what one feels."
— Gustave Flaubert

"Here I am trying to live, or rather, I am trying to teach
the death within me how to live."
— Jean Cocteau

"I am not proud, but I am happy; and happiness blinds,
I think, more than pride."
— Alexandre Dumas,
The Count of Monte Cristo

"Even the darkest night will end and the sun will rise."
— Victor Hugo, **Les Misérables**

"Blow the candle out, I don't need to see what my
thoughts look like."
— Émile Zola, **Germinal**

"The idea which tyrants find most useful is the idea of God."
— Stendhal

sorrow

sorrow

*"And remember: you must never, under any circumstances,
despair. To hope and to act, these are our duties
in misfortune."*
— Boris Pasternak, **Doctor Zhivago**

*"Are the days of winter sunshine just as sad for you, too?
When it is misty, in the evenings, and I am out walking by
myself, it seems to me that the rain is falling through my
heart and causing it to crumble into ruins."*
— Gustave Flaubert

"Our sweetest songs are those of saddest thought."
— Percy Bysshe Shelley

"I will find new meaning in every joy and sorrow."
— Jalaluddin Rumi

*"More tears are shed over answered prayers than
unanswered ones."*
— Truman Capote

*"It is often hard to bear the tears that we ourselves
have caused."*
— Marcel Proust

*"Deep in earth my love is lying
And I must weep alone."*
— Edgar Allan Poe

*"Nobody deserves your tears, but whoever deserves them
will not make you cry."*
— Gabriel Garcia Marquez

"We need never be ashamed of our tears."
*— Charles Dickens, **Great Expectations***

"The end is in the beginning and yet you go on."
*— Samuel Beckett, **Endgame***

*"Is your face a beautiful blossom or a sweet torture?
I have no complaints but my heart is tempted to let you
hear of its sorrows."*
— Jalaluddin Rumi

*"Every man has his secret sorrows which the world knows
not; and often times we call a man cold when he
is only sad."*
— Henry Wadsworth Longfellow

*"They say when you are missing someone that they are
probably feeling the same, but I don't think it's possible for
you to miss me as much as I'm missing you right now."*
— Edna St. Vincent Millay

*"Nothing can cure the soul but the senses, just as nothing
can cure the senses but the soul."*
*— Oscar Wilde, **The Picture of Dorian Gray***

"No one ever told me that grief felt so like fear."
*— C.S. Lewis, **A Grief Observed***

solitude

solitude

*"Little as she was addicted to solitude, there had come to
be moments when it seemed a welcome escape
from the empty noises of her life."*
— *Edith Wharton,* **The House of Mirth**

"I long for solitude and yet I cannot stand it."
— *Eugène Ionesco*

*"Solitude is fine but you need someone to tell that
solitude is fine."*
— *Honoré de Balzac*

*"There are days when solitude is a heady wine that
intoxicates you with freedom, others when it is a bitter
tonic, and still others when it is a poison that makes you
beat your head against the wall."*
— *Colette*

*"I care for myself. The more solitary, the more friendless,
the more unsustained I am, the more I will respect myself."*
— *Charlotte Brontë,* **Jane Eyre**

*"Who hears music, feels his solitude
Peopled at once."*
— *Robert Browning*

"Solitude sometimes is best society."
— *John Milton,* **Paradise Lost**

*"Only the solitary seek the truth, and they break with
all those who don't love it sufficiently."*
— *Boris Pasternak,* **Doctor Zhivago**

*"Solitude produces originality, bold and astonishing beauty,
poetry. But solitude also produces perverseness, the
disproportionate, the absurd and the forbidden."*
— *Thomas Mann*

*"A poet is a nightingale who sits in darkness and sings to
cheer its own solitude with sweet sounds."*
— *Percy Bysshe Shelley*

*"The more powerful and original a mind, the more it will
incline towards the religion of solitude."*
— *Aldous Huxley*

*"I live in that solitude which is painful in youth, but delicious
in the years of maturity."*
— *Albert Einstein*

*"Whosoever is delighted in solitude, is either a wild beast
or a god."*
— *Aristotle*

*"Then stirs the feeling infinite, so felt
In solitude, where we are least alone."*
— *George Gordon, Lord Byron*

*"There is no insurmountable solitude. All paths lead to the
same goal: to convey to others what we are."*
— *Pablo Neruda*

on living...

on living...

"It is nothing to die. It is frightful not to live."
— *Victor Hugo,* **Les Misérables**

*"It's necessary to have wished for death in order to know
how good it is to live."*
— *Alexandre Dumas,*
The Count of Monte Cristo

*"The living owe it to those who no longer can speak to tell
their story for them."*
— *Czesław Miłosz,* **The Issa Valley**

*"A writer never has a vacation. For a writer, life consists
of either writing or thinking about writing."*
— *Eugène Ionesco*

"Life is simply what our feelings do to us."
— *Honoré de Balzac*

*"The body is wiser than its inhabitants. The body is the soul.
The body is God's messenger."*
— *Erica Jong*

"Life is an awful, ugly place to not have a best friend."
— *Sarah Dessen,* **Someone Like You**

"Live to the point of tears."
— *Albert Camus*

"It's a very funny thing about life; if you refuse to accept anything but the best, you very often get it."
— W. Somerset Maugham

"I wonder how many people I've looked at all my life and never seen."
— John Steinbeck,
The Winter of Our Discontent

"The mass of men lead lives of quiet desperation."
— Henry David Thoreau, **Walden**

"I don't know if I should care for a man who made life easy; I should want someone who made it interesting."
— Edith Wharton

"Life is a storm, my young friend. You will bask in the sunlight one moment, be shattered on the rocks the next. What makes you a man is what you do when that storm comes."
— Alexandre Dumas

"It is better to be hated for what you are than to be loved for what you are not."
— André Gide, **Autumn Leaves**

"A woman has to live her life, or live to repent not having lived it."
— D.H. Lawrence,
Lady Chatterley's Lover

truths & illusions

truths & illusions

"If the sky could dream, it would dream of dragons."
— *Ilona Andrews,* **Fate's Edge**

"Humankind cannot bear very much reality."
— *T.S. Eliot,* **Four Quartets**

"For truth is always strange; stranger than fiction."
— *George Gordon, Lord Byron*

"There are some things one remembers even though they may never have happened."
— *Harold Pinter,* **Old Times**

"Never touch your idols: the gilding will stick to your fingers."
— *Gustave Flaubert,* **Madame Bovary**

"Why do we call all our generous ideas illusions, and the mean ones truths?"
— *Edith Wharton,* **The House of Mirth**

"I don't want realism. I want magic! Yes, yes, magic! I try to give that to people. I misrepresent things to them. I don't tell the truth, I tell what ought to be the truth. And it that's sinful, then let me be damned for it!"
— *Tennessee Williams,*
A Streetcar Named Desire

"Believe those who are seeking the truth. Doubt those who find it."
— André Gide

"The sole substitute for an experience we have not ourselves lived through is art and literature."
— Aleksandr Solzhenitsyn

"He who is conceived in a cage yearns for the cage."
— Yevgeny Yevtushenko

"If you cannot get rid of the family skeleton, you may as well make it dance."
— George Bernard Shaw, **Immaturity**

"How should we be able to forget those myths that are at the beginning of all peoples, the myths about dragons that at the last moment turn into princesses; perhaps all the dragons in our lives are princesses who are only waiting to see us act, just once, with beauty and courage. Perhaps everything that frightens us is, in its deepest essence, something helpless that wants our love."
— Rainer Maria Rilke

"A great deal of intelligence can be invested in ignorance when the need for illusion is deep."
— Saul Bellow

"There is an old illusion. It is called good and evil."
— Friedrich Nietzsche

on being a writer

on being a writer

"I always find it more difficult to say the things I mean than the things I don't."
— W. Somerset Maugham, **The Painted Veil**

"I would rather be attacked than unnoticed. For the worst thing you can do to an author is to be silent as to his works."
— Samuel Johnson

"You can't wait for inspiration. You have to go after it with a club."
— Jack London

"How vain it is to sit down to write when you have not stood up to live."
— Henry David Thoreau

"A man of genius makes no mistakes. His errors are volitional and are the portals of discovery."
— James Joyce, **Ulysses**

"We work in the dark...we do what we can. We give what we have. Our doubt is our passion, and our passion is our task. The rest is the madness of art."
— Henry James, **The Middle Years**

"The poet doesn't invent. He listens."
— Jean Cocteau

"All you have to do is write one true sentence. Write the truest sentence that you know."
— Ernest Hemingway

"Write a little every day, without hope, without despair."
— Karen Blixen

"The artist is nothing without the gift, but the gift is nothing without work."
— Émile Zola

"Shut your eyes and see."
— James Joyce

"I am a galley slave to pen and ink."
— Honoré de Balzac

*"Good, better, best
Never let it rest,
Till your good is better
And better is best."*
— Thomas Hardy

"Everyone has talent. What's rare is the courage to follow it to the dark places where it leads."
— Erica Jong

"There are three rules for writing a novel. Unfortunately, no one knows what they are."
— W. Somerset Maugham

courage & fear

courage & fear

"Fear urged him to go back, but growth drove him on."
— Jack London, **White Fang**

"It takes courage to grow up and become who you really are."
— e.e. cummings

"Our greatest fears lie in anticipation."
— Honoré de Balzac

"You cannot swim for new horizons until you have courage to lose sight of the shore."
— William Faulkner

"One doesn't discover new lands without consenting to lose sight, for a very long time, of the shore."
— André Gide

"Courage is resistance to fear, mastery of fear — not absence of fear."
— Mark Twain

"Although the road is never ending, take a step and keep walking, do not look fearfully into the distance...On this path let your heart be your guide, for the body is hesitant and full of fear."
— Jalaluddin Rumi

"Courage is found in unlikely places."
— *J.R.R. Tolkien*

"Courage is knowing what not to fear."
— *Plato*

"Courage is grace under pressure."
— *Ernest Hemingway*

"Never laugh at live dragons."
— *J.R.R. Tolkien*

"Fearing no insult, asking for no crown, receive with indifference both flattery and slander, and do not argue with a fool."
— *Aleksandr Pushkin*

"I have not ceased being fearful, but I have ceased to let fear control me."
— *Erica Jong*

"Freedom lies in being bold."
— *Robert Frost*

"It is curious that physical courage should be so common in the world and moral courage so rare."
— *Mark Twain*

"A patriot must always be ready to defend his country against his government."
— *Edward Abbey*

unforgettable

unforgettable

*"If history were taught in the form of stories, it would
never be forgotten."*
— Rudyard Kipling, **The Collected Works**

"Education doesn't make you smarter."
— Aleksandr Solzhenitsyn

*"Sit, be still, and listen,
because you're drunk
and we're at
the edge of the roof."*
— Jalaluddin Rumi

"Forever is composed of nows."
— Emily Dickinson

*"Hypocrisy is a fashionable vice, and all fashionable vices
pass for virtue."*
— Molière

*"There is no such thing as a great talent without great
willpower."*
— Honoré de Balzac

*"The greatest masterpiece in literature is only a dictionary
out of order."*
— Jean Cocteau

"What the public criticizes in you, cultivate. It is you."
— *Jean Cocteau*

"A man's silence is wonderful to listen to."
— *Thomas Hardy*

"The superiority of one man's opinion over another's is never so great as when the opinion is about a woman."
— *Henry James*

"Youth is wasted on the young."
— *George Bernard Shaw*

"O lost,
And by the wind grieved,
Ghost,
Come back again."
— *Thomas Wolfe,*
Look Homeward, Angel

"Advice is what we ask for when we already know the answer but wish we didn't."
— *Erica Jong*

"Another belief of mine: that everyone else my age is an adult, whereas I am merely in disguise."
— *Margaret Atwood,* **Cat's Eye**

"All great and precious things are lonely."
— *John Steinbeck,* **East of Eden**

the Europeans

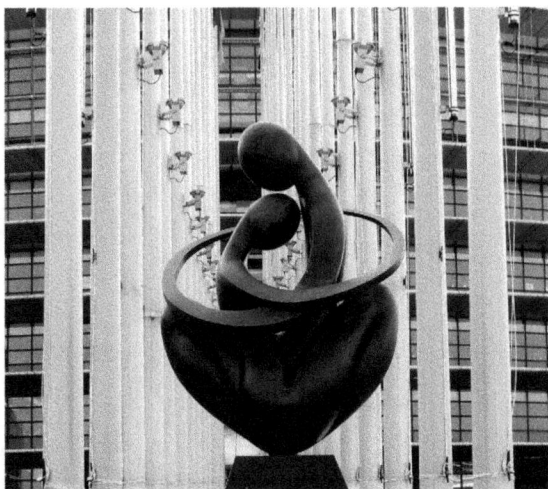

the Europeans

"You can easily judge the character of a man by how he treats those who can do nothing for him."
— Johann Wolfgang von Goethe

"There are so many different kinds of stupidity, and cleverness is one of the worst."
— Thomas Mann,
The Magic Mountain

"The joke loses everything when the joker laughs himself."
— Friedrich Schiller

"There is nothing in the world so irresistibly contagious as laughter and good humor."
— Charles Dickens, **A Christmas Carol**

"You are the music while the music lasts."
— T.S. Eliot

"It infuriates me to be wrong when I know I'm right."
— Molière

"The road to Hell is paved with good intentions."
— Samuel Johnson

"It is not the answer that enlightens, but the question."
— Eugène Ionesco

"Our worst misfortunes never happen, and most miseries
lie in anticipation."
— *Honoré de Balzac*

"Common sense is not so common."
— *Voltaire*

"I am a lie that always speaks the truth."
— *Jean Cocteau*

"I was a great believer in hot buttered toast at all hours
of the day."
— *Frank O'Connor,* **Collected Stories**

"It takes a great deal of history to produce a little literature."
— *Henry James*

"I intend to judge things for myself; to judge wrongly,
I think, is more honorable than not to judge at all."
— *Henry James*

"O God, make me good, but not yet."
— *Evelyn Waugh,* **Brideshead Revisited**

"Not that I want to be a god or a hero. Just to change into
a tree, grow for ages, not hurt anyone."
— *Czesław Miłosz*

"To achieve harmony in bad taste is the height of elegance."
— *Jean Genet*

thoughts...

thoughts...

"If I got rid of my demons, I'd lose my angels."
— *Tennessee Williams*

"Life shrinks or expands in proportion to one's courage."
— *Anaïs Nin*

*"Life is not always a matter of holding good cards, but
sometimes, playing a poor hand well."*
— *Jack London*

*"To be left alone is the most precious thing one can
ask of the modern world."*
— *Anthony Burgess*

*"I always prefer to believe the best of everybody; it saves
so much trouble."*
— *Rudyard Kipling*

"This world is but canvas to our imaginations."
— *Henry David Thoreau*

"What deep wounds ever closed without a scar?"
— *George Gordon, Lord Byron*

"My books, at any rate, deserve to be burned."
— *Alfred Doblin*

"I have possessed that heart, that noble soul, in whose presence I seemed to be more than I really was, because I was all that I could be."
— Johann Wolfgang von Goethe

"Laughter is a sunbeam of the soul."
— Thomas Mann, **The Magic Mountain**

"To save all we must risk all."
— Friedrich Schiller

"We turn not older with years but newer every day."
— Emily Dickinson

"She had no tolerance for scenes which were not of her own making."
— Edith Wharton, **The House of Mirth**

"Oh, what a love it was, utterly free, unique, like nothing else on earth! Their thoughts were like other people's songs."
— Boris Pasternak, **Doctor Zhivago**

"As a general rule...people ask for advice only in order not to follow it; or if they do follow it, in order to have someone to blame for giving it."
— Alexandre Dumas

"Sometimes things become possible if we want them bad enough."
— T.S. Eliot

advice

advice

*"It is not only what we do, but also what we do not do,
for which we are accountable."*
— Molière

*"A novelist has to know enough about a subject to fool the
passenger next to him on an airplane."*
— David Foster Wallace

*"The friend who holds your hand and says the wrong thing
is made of dearer stuff than the one who stays away."*
— Barbara Kingsolver

"A friend to all is a friend to none."
— Aristotle

*"A man can never have too much red wine, too many books,
or too much ammunition."*
— Rudyard Kipling

*"Nature makes only dumb animals. We owe the fools
to society."*
— Honoré de Balzac

"Hope is not found in a way out but a way through."
— Robert Frost

"Success and failure are equally disastrous."
— Tennessee Williams

"To have joy, one must share it."
— *George Gordon, Lord Byron*

"Dare to err and to dream."
— *Friedrich Schiller*

"As soon as you trust yourself, you will know how to live."
— *Johann Wolfgang von Goethe*

"For all evils, there are two remedies: time and silence."
— *Alexandre Dumas,*
The Count of Monte Cristo

"Only those who will risk going too far can possibly find out how far one can go."
— *T.S. Eliot*

"To put everything in balance is good, to put everything in harmony is better."
— *Victor Hugo*

"Suspect each moment, for it is a thief, tiptoeing away with more than it brings."
— *John Updike,* **A Month of Sundays**

"Try to be a rainbow in someone's cloud."
— *Maya Angelou,* **Letter to My Daughter**

"Say what you have to say, not what you ought. Any truth is better than make-believe."
— *Henry David Thoreau*

poetry & the poets

poetry & the poets

"Love is the poetry of the senses."
— Honoré de Balzac

"The purpose of poetry is to remind us how difficult it is to
remain just one person..."
— Czesław Miłosz

"Poetry is when an emotion has found its thought and the
thought has found words."
— Robert Frost

"Poetry and art are the breath of life to her."
— Edith Wharton, **The Age of Innocence**

"Can you remember who you were, before the world
told you who you should be?"
— Charles Bukowski

"Heart, we will forget him,
You and I, tonight!
You must forget the warmth he gave,
I will forget the light."
— Emily Dickinson

"There will be time, there will be time
To prepare a face to meet the faces that you meet."
— T.S. Eliot

"That which God said to the rose,
and caused it to laugh in full-blown beauty,
He said to my heart,
and made it a hundred times more beautiful."
— Jalaluddin Rumi

"The sunlight claps the earth, and the moonbeams kiss the
sea: what are all these kissings worth, if thou kiss not me?"
— Percy Bysshe Shelley

"From the ashes, a fire shall be woken,
A light from the shadows shall spring;
Renewed shall be blade that was broken,
The crownless again shall be king."
— J.R.R. Tolkien,
The Fellowship of the Ring

"There is but one task for all —
One life for each to give.
What stands if Freedom fall?"
— Rudyard Kipling, **Complete Verse**

"I am ashes where once I was fire..."
— George Gordon, Lord Byron

"And the Raven, never flitting,
still is sitting, still is sitting
On the pallid bust of Pallas
just above my chamber door..."
— Edgar Allan Poe

life & truth

life & truth

"To live is so startling it leaves little time for anything else."
— Emily Dickinson

"The truth isn't always beauty, but the hunger for it is."
— Nadine Gordimer

*"The happiest miser on earth is the man who saves up
every friend he can make."*
— Robert E. Sherwood

"A learned fool is more a fool than an ignorant fool."
— Molière

*"One can be very much in love with a woman without
wishing to spend the rest of one's life with her."*
*— W. Somerset Maugham, **The Painted Veil***

"Love truth, but pardon error."
— Voltaire

*"Take your life in your own hands, and what happens?
A terrible thing: no one to blame."*
— Erica Jong

*"Everything in the universe is within you. Ask all from
yourself."*
— Jalaluddin Rumi

"Life cannot go on without a great deal of forgetting."
— *Honoré de Balzac,* **Cousin Bette**

*"In a room where people unanimously maintain
a conspiracy of silence, one word of truth
sounds like a pistol shot."*
— *Czesław Miłosz*

"On what slender threads do life and fortune hang."
— *Alexandre Dumas*

"Rather than love, than money, than fame, give me truth."
— *Henry David Thoreau,* **Walden**

*"The greatest happiness of life is the conviction that we
are loved — for ourselves, or rather, loved in spite
of ourselves."*
— *Victor Hugo*

"Truth is so rare, it is delightful to tell it."
— *Emily Dickinson*

*"A thing is not necessarily true because a man
dies for it."*
— *Oscar Wilde*

"The only truth is music."
— *Jack Kerouac*

dark

dark

"No matter how fast light travels, it finds the darkness has always got there first, and is waiting for it."
— *Terry Pratchett*

"There comes a time when you look into the mirror and you realize what you see is all that you will ever be. And then you accept it. Or kill yourself. Or stop looking in mirrors."
— *Tennessee Williams*

"Do not go gentle into that good night, Old age should burn and rave at close of day..."
— *Dylan Thomas*

"It looked as if a night of dark intent was coming, and not only a night, an age."
— *Robert Frost*

"When it is dark enough, you can see the stars."
— *Ralph Waldo Emerson*

"Now that I am without you, all is desolate; All that was once so beautiful is dead..."
— *Conrad Aiken*

"I knew nothing but shadows and I thought them to be real."
— *Oscar Wilde,* **The Picture of Dorian Gray**

"When I am dead, my dearest,
Sing no sad songs for me;
Plant thou no roses at my head,
Nor shady cypress tree..."
— *Christina Rossetti*

"Of our forgetfulness until we find
It becomes strangely easy to forgive
Even ourselves with this clouding of the mind,
This cinerous blur and smudge in which we live."
— *Anthony Hecht*

"I am terrified by this dark thing that sleeps in me."
— *Sylvia Plath*

"Whoever is not in his coffin and the dark grave, let him
know he has enough."
— *Walt Whitman*

"Without darkness, nothing comes to birth, As without
light, nothing flowers."
— *May Sarton*

"I like the night. Without the dark, we'd never see the stars."
— *Stephenie Meyer,*
Twilight

"Darkness is your candle."
— *Jalaluddin Rumi*

light

light

"We can easily forgive a child who is afraid of the dark;
the real tragedy of life is when men are afraid of the light."
— *Plato*

"The hardest thing to explain is the glaringly evident which
everybody has decided not to see."
— *Ayn Rand,* **The Fountainhead**

"The wound is the place where the Light enters you."
— *Jalaluddin Rumi*

"Every moment of light and dark is a miracle."
— *Walt Whitman*

"There are two kinds of light — the glow that illuminates,
and the glare that obscures."
— *James Thurber*

"There are darknesses in life and there are lights, and you
are one of the lights, the light of all lights."
— *Bram Stoker,* **Dracula**

"There is a crack in everything.
That's how the light gets in."
— *Leonard Cohen*

"Moonlight drowns out all but the brightest stars."
— *J.R.R. Tolkien,* **The Lord of the Rings**

"Man reading should be man intensely alive. The book should be a ball of light in one's hand."
— *Ezra Pound*

"...We see the light that fractures through unquiet water. We see the light but see not whence it comes..."
— *T.S. Eliot*

"Love is the longing for the half of ourselves we have lost."
— *Milan Kundera,*
The Unbearable Lightness of Being

"How far that little candle throws his beams! So shines a good deed in a weary world."
— *William Shakespeare,* **The Merchant of Venice**

"Long is the way and hard, that out of Hell leads up to light."
— *John Milton,* **Paradise Lost**

"In the moonlight, which is always sad, as the light of the sun itself is — as the light called human life is, at its coming and its going."
— *Charles Dickens,* **A Tale of Two Cities**

"A beautiful book is a victory won in all the battlefields of human thought."
— *Honoré de Balzac*

"We are so scared of being judged that we look for every excuse to procrastinate."
— *Erica Jong*

afterword

When I was a child, reading was my only escape from family wars. The highlight of my week was our shopping trip to the grocer that sold 'Classics Illustrated'. Dumas, Stevenson, Eliot, Dickens, Hugo, Kipling, Shelley, Wells, transported me to incredible places and times far away from my troubles. I never dreamed one day I would leave that miserable town and become a writer myself, living in a beautiful European city so much like the ones I discovered in my books a thousand years ago.

I still remember lines from my early reading and many are included in this book. I love how a few well-crafted words can create a world within a reader's mind. Whenever I find myself rewriting a sentence too many times, I retrieve one of my classics and read random lines...words from the past become torches that light my way.

I hope this book of quotations inspires your own writing, your own life...if you need other worlds to find peace in even for a little while, as I once did.

— *Kimberly Coleman*
Dublin, Ireland

Also available from your local bookseller or
order the title from worldwide Amazon!

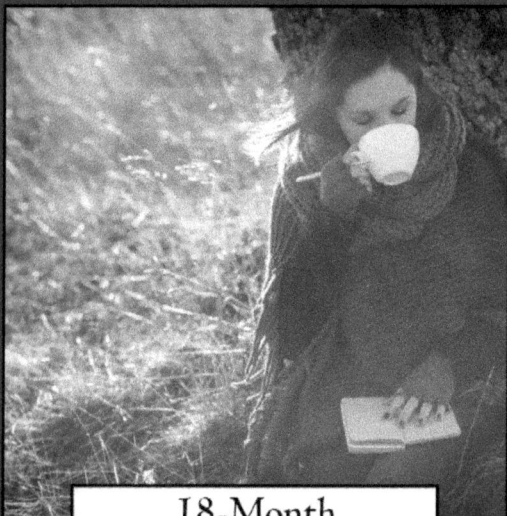

18-Month
Calendar For Writers

July 2017 -
December 2018
QUOTES AND INSPIRATION

KIMBERLY COLEMAN

www.ingramcontent.com/pod-product-compliance
Lightning Source LLC
Chambersburg PA
CBHW060312030426
42336CB00011B/1008